A CEO Playbook

THE CRAFT

Secret Codes and Methods for Unlocking Exponential Financial Value

CHRIS MAILANDER

ISBN-13: 978-1-7325624-2-4

Book Formatting by Kristen Forbes (deviancepress.com)

To Elizabeth, my wife, who puts up with all of this.

The truth lies in the secrets we shroud.

CONTENTS

Download the Audiobook for Free

We do some of our best thinking while on a flight, driving to work, or on the treadmill.

These are our moments to dream, aspire, and contemplate.

It is where we develop our long-term vision and the strategies for getting there.

As a thank you for buying *The Craft*, please accept as my gift the audiobook version for free.

To download the audiobook for free, go to:

http://ChrisMailander.com/TheCraft/audiobook

PRELUDE

You stand at the helm.
They are depending on you.
Your employees. Your investors.
Their families and yours.

They trust you can create.
They trust you can see around corners.

They trust you can take them places they cannot otherwise go.

There are those who are able to find the "something greater"
hiding in the darkness just beyond.
They possess something intangible, elusive, and ephemeral.
They see, sense, and think differently.
They know secrets.
They are masters of *The Craft*.
They are the ones we trust to take us places we cannot
otherwise go.

WHO SHOULD READ THIS BOOK

The Craft is for those we entrust to find the path.

It is for those executives—CEOs, COOs, CFOs, general counsels, EVPs, SVPs—who are competing in a world that is just flat-out moving faster and where

the stakes are higher,

they must steward organizations that have grown more complex,

new threats can gut their businesses with blazing speed, and

the outcomes are more unforgiving.

The Craft is for those who own responsibility for those decisions that succeed—and fail.

It is for those whose responsibility is to successfully navigate the critical inflection points the company will face—the next big deal, the exit, the crisis, the reorganization, the investment, the launch—that will define everything that comes next for their companies.

It is for those who know there are secrets.

They are revealed to all.

They can be heard, sensed, and understood by only a few.

It is for these few to access the codes that unlock their companies' exponential financial value.

WHY I WROTE THIS BOOK

I have worked across five continents and in nine industries helping CEOs, national political leaders, and global investors navigate their most critical moments.

This work has been both in the boardroom and in the trenches. In big companies and small. With companies on their heels and those on the attack. It has included those who make the front page and others who prefer the shadows.

It has involved the corporate art form of harnessing the full potential of diverse networks of stakeholders operating across complex ecosystems—mustering their way toward a common business objective while wrestling through the messy tangle of human nature that influences the journey there.

It has involved standing with those charged with making a singular decision before them:

Is this a go or a no go?

It has enabled me to witness when people perform at their best. And their worst.

Through it all, I have been decoding the mysteries that lie just below the waterline of the fray taking place above, asking why.

The Craft reflects the lessons that can be learned only by looking directly into the eyes of those who stand in their most critical moments, seeking passage through the darkened door before them. Once opened, it will determine everything that comes next. For better or for worse.

I wrote this book to share these lessons with corporate executives and leaders who now face their own critical moments—the ones that will determine everything that comes next. Prepare to make these moments your best.

HOW TO USE THIS BOOK

We all have those moments when we ask, "What now?"

When we encounter something new that we haven't experienced before.

When something isn't playing out the way we thought it should.

When those who are sitting across the table from us—prospective partners, vendors, financiers, employees, advisers—aren't saying the things we thought they would say or doing the things they said they would do.

When we've been executing our strategy—day over day—and then it lurches, loses momentum, hits a roadblock, or is at risk of running off the rails.

"What now?"

The Craft is for you in these moments

> when you need a tick list to remember what you might have missed,

> as a source of creative inspiration to break through the logjam or reignite the fire beneath your critical initiative,

> for clues to decoding why others are doing what they are doing, or

> as a playbook to unlock the exponential financial value harboring within your company.

In moments like this, we often feel the butterflies in our stomachs. It is the feeling that percolates up when we are looking for answers and are asking, "What now?"

It is fueled by our desire to create tremendous value, do right, ring the bell, and leave a mark—the kind of mark others will say, "There, that was it! That is when the company really took off."

When you feel moments like this, use the methodology of *The Craft*.

Let it be your guide, your tick list, your playbook, your inspiration, your insight, and your advantage.

Find answers where others do not know to look.

Take them places they cannot otherwise go.

PART 1

FOUNDATION

1

WHAT IT WILL LOOK LIKE

Many CEOs imagine their performance in their most critical moments.

They will be warriors in the arena.

They move deftly, powerfully, fending off the attacks. The short jabs, the thrust from the blindside, the long-reaching arc of the javelin thrown.

The crowds roar.

They leave victorious.

History will regale their brilliance and cunning.

It will be glorious.

2

THEY WILL MARK THE POINT

In the life of a company, there will be certain inflection points that define it.

These are the events we will look back on, excitedly point to, and say, "There, that was it! That was the point when the company really took off."

Indeed, it will be glorious.

Just as easily, however, we can point to events on that timeline that mark the beginning of the end. Where the trajectory of the company just never recovered. It flattened. Or it fell away.

We point to the bad decisions made—or, often, to the absence of a decision—that left the company sputtering, wounded and weak.

Within these critical inflection points, everything changes:

The rules change.

People behave differently.

The noise, confusion, and pressure intensify the experience.

Perception is distorted.

Reactions become more volatile.

Rational thinkers become irrational actors in a play they cannot control.

There is a fundamental shift—neurologically, emotionally, and physiologically.

In these moments, opportunities are lost, mistakes are made, and everything that comes next for the business becomes something different. Often it is less.

These are the moments when you gasp, shake your head, and ask, "What were they thinking?"

Often the answer is, "They weren't."

3

FILM ROOM

I wish there were game film on CEOs.

I wish I could spend the week studying the tape to see how they behave in different situations, as the conditions wax and wane, when the rules change—sometimes suddenly, sometimes subtly.

I want to roll the film in slow motion to study how they get their read—what they see, what they anticipate, and what they miss. I want to know how to put pressure on them, box them in, and force errors. I want to decode their tells—the little clues that indicate what they will do next.

I wish I could then sit with them in a darkened room and break it down, revealing the aha moments and refining the techniques.

But you don't find game film on CEOs.

They make their decisions in walled-off conference rooms. You have to pass through a secure entrance to get there. There is a confidentiality agreement that entrusted you to see the sausage being made—and not reveal these secrets.

Those who do see CEOs in critical moments—working with them elbow to elbow in those moments that will define the future of the company from that point forward—aren't always able to coach up and help their bosses get it right. There are limits. It isn't always prudent. They do the best they can.

Often, it is not enough.

So the patterns repeat. The diligent executive will suffer from the same blind spots. They will react to the same triggers. They will give away what they will do next by showing the same tell.

If there were game film, I could point to those moments when they were

> stalling,

> hesitating or hedging,

> making decisions that gave away their power,

> painting the company into a box, or

> leaving money on the table.

The film would show when the CEO was losing

the power to shape the future by their vision, words, and action;

the command of the moment;

the trust of others; and

the ability to create exponential financial value.

4

WHAT ISN'T BEING SAID

The calls I get usually come in the same way. There is a pattern. It will repeat.

I will be briefed on the substantive issues, addressing the challenges in the financials, strategy, market timing, competitive landscape, technology, sales, or whatever else is believed to be holding the company back. It is logical. It is where we are told the problems always lie.

Then there is a subtle shift.

To be quite honest, for the longest time, I couldn't feel it. It took me nearly three decades to learn it. It took three corporate spinouts, an IPO, architecting and negotiating several billion dollars of deals across five continents, rebuilding businesses after the bubble popped in 2002 and then again in 2008, and working in war zones after 9/11. It took incubating dozens of new corporate ventures—starting some up, believing in them all, giving blood, and then recognizing most must be culled with Darwinistic brutality. It took building complex delivery and operational ecosystems around companies with the potential to unlock significant financial value, realize massive operational efficiencies, and innovate their way to a greater and enduring potential for the long term.

Along the way, it always involved knitting together the vivid tapestry of partners, vendors, lawyers, management consultants, systems integrators, technologists, marketers, communicators, financiers, policy makers, and others necessary to actually realize such financial and strategic value.

Then, at the tip of the spear of all this have been the individual executives standing in their most critical moments. When the pressure has been most intense. When their responsibility has been at its greatest. It has included the thousands I've worked with who have run financial institutions, investment funds, health-care and pharmaceutical companies, telecom companies and tech companies, agencies of the US government, and, quite literally, nations. They have been the anointed stewards we have entrusted to attain our most critical objectives under the most challenging of circumstances.

As a product of these experiences, I now can sense when that subtle shift occurs. When I feel it, I can anticipate what comes next.

It begins when they struggle with what to say, how to say it, or whether to say it at all.

By this point in our conversation, they've listed for me all the things they were told would lead to success but didn't:

The big deal should have closed by now.

The new brand should have launched by now.

The partnership should have blossomed by now.

The reorg should have been done by now.

The crisis should have been averted by now.

In the midst of what is shifting, I'm listening for what it is they don't say.

Some offer me what they can, but it is only a peephole's view into the circus inside. They lack a language for describing what holds them back.

Others just don't know. They haven't seen this before, and they haven't felt it before.

Others seem to know of the problem, but they won't say it. It may be embarrassing. It may be painful. They would like to keep the secrets safely stashed away, hidden.

Their lack of words or understanding—or desire to hide— reveals the first truth. What they are really asking is, "What now?"

The second truth that emerges in this first call is that the executive knows they are at risk of making a bad decision when it could matter most—one that could be the first domino in a chain leading to

windows of opportunity closing;

problems locking in and festering;

the company losing financial value;

employees, investors, their families, and others suffering; and

legacies going up in smoke.

Finally, there is a third truth that will be revealed: they didn't call me first but last.

By the time I get that call, they've run this path as far as they could.

All the smart guys have already weighed in. They did their best. They meant well.

It just isn't working.

When I get the call—when they feel boxed in, stuck, under pressure, or at their greatest risk of getting the decision wrong and tipping over the first domino that defines everything that comes after—what they are asking for is magic.

They hope I have it.

5

MAGIC

The last call leads to the first visit.

I will fly somewhere quickly, without much time to prepare. I will go to a gray tower or office park and check in with security. They will issue me a sticky name tag with an unrecognizable headshot of me on it. I won't place it on my lapel but instead put it in my pocket. Not once has anyone cared. I'll take the elevator, get off at the assigned floor, pass through some glass doors. Someone will usher me into a conference room. There will be between three and twelve people in that conference room. There will be an empty chair. Sometimes it is at the head of the table. Sometimes it is along the side.

When I walk into that conference room for the first time, I can see it in their eyes. The strangers assembled have so much hope. They hope I have answers. They hope I have a new way of thinking about their problem. They hope I can find a crack of light.

In that moment, when we are still strangers, when nothing yet is really known, when we all have a few jitters we can feel in our bellies, I am at my most powerful. It is because they believe in magic.

The expensive gurus have set the strategy and messaging. The smart guys have built the financials. The lawyers have negotiated the terms. They've spent a fortune just to get here. And it isn't working.

What they need now is magic.

And the good stuff.

This power is fleeting. Hope is so fragile. It can be lost in a moment. The magician cannot drop a card. Or tug at their pocket. Or look to the wrong point. Not a single misstep. They have hope.

I have to deliver.

Once the clock starts, I won't see things as clearly as in that first moment.

They will tell me their story. They will tell me what they will want me to know and try to hide what they do not.

They will focus on those who are frustrating their objective— the counterparties who won't improve the deal terms, a reporter who has an agenda, a dispute with someone who "just doesn't get it." Their lens points out. Often, it should be pointed in.

I know that my purpose will be to figure out a way to break a stalemate, get parties back to the table, find a new approach or a new argument, or inflect the value of a deal up in their favor.

But in this moment, the deal terms, pricing, or what someone else is doing to them—blocking, fighting, ghosting, demanding, failing—is not important to the magic that needs to be immediately performed. The magic is not out there.

Instead, I need to sense how these strangers are perceiving, reacting, and thinking. The magic is in here. It will be found within those hearts and minds gathered in this moment, asking, "What now?"

Shifting how someone perceives, reacts, and thinks in times like this is the path that creates financial value.

It gets the deal done.

It gives birth to a new innovation.

It remaps how the actors in the drama interplay.

It puts the company onto a new arc.

This is where I will find the magic they covet. In gray conference rooms. With strangers.

Who have hope.

6

UNLOCKING EXPONENTIAL VALUE

Successfully unlocking exponential financial value is the product of decoding, transcribing, and integrating the insights gained at each of six distinct stages in a company's journey.

Most companies only do three and a half, maybe four. Five if they are crushing it.

It is a problem.

First, although they may generate sufficient returns to justify their actions over the short term, they will not unlock exponential financial value.

Second, their probability of success in pursuing their growth, innovation, and transformation strategies will be low. They will fail because their strategies are typical and logical but not well crafted. They may never even know why. They will be flummoxed. Maybe they were just doing what they had done in the past. Perhaps they will simply have done what their advisers told them. Or, like many executives, perhaps they simply set the trajectory of their path to realize sufficient financial returns to justify their actions with their boards, shareholders, employees, and themselves, but they have come up short in finding the path that leads to exponential returns. Under any of these scenarios, what they have done is simply kick the can, buying time until the next CEO takes over the reins or the market inflects again. Then, if the pattern repeats itself, as it most often does, they will predictably retrench into what will be whispered near the watercooler as another round of navel-gazing.

Although some of the rules of the game may in fact be changing with the accelerating pace of corporate adaptation and evolution, one rule will remain the same: kicking the can is a short-lived game.

The reality is that all companies—from the largest to the smallest, from multinationals to midmarket leaders to entrepreneurial innovators—are living beasts. As such, they must adapt and evolve in response to the conditions they face or get out of the way. This process of corporate adaptation and evolution is no longer measured in decades or even in three to five years. Instead, it is compressing, year over year, quarter over quarter, month over month. The process of adaptation and evolution must also, therefore, necessarily compress—year over year, quarter over quarter, month over month.

Senior executives who think in linear, routine, and even the predictable ways that served them so well a decade ago, but who are not able to now create, innovate, transform, disrupt, and win in a game moving at the faster and faster pace demanded by today's competitive market, will slough off slowly or simply die. In fact, the majority of today's major corporations will no longer exist in a decade or two. They cannot keep pace. They will not move fast enough. They cannot see, sense and envision what lies in wait ahead. Their fate is inevitable. Perhaps it is even predetermined. Others—some of which haven't even begun to breathe—will take their place. There are deeper codes that explain why.

To not only compete and survive but also to win by growing, innovating, transforming, adapting and evolving to meet the needs of what lies in the future requires understanding those codes that truly make the corporate organism stronger, more resilient, more advanced, and more intelligent. These codes lie deeply within the organism. Know where to look. Know what you are looking for. Know what to do when you find them.

Here's how.

The Craft involves deepening the body of insight into and understanding of the full set of variables that directly affect the ability of a company to truly unlock exponential financial value.

Illustration 1

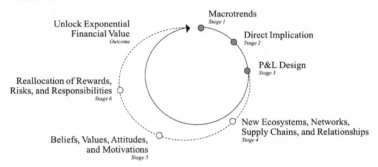

Macrotrends (Stage 1)

This is where we begin.

All the big conferences focus on it. The trendy podcasts all talk about it. It is the buzz they inject into the business headlines. Innovation, disruption, new business models, disintermediation, transformation, growth, and the endless prognostications about those who get it and those who never will.

Every company in every vertical market is affected by transformative macrotrends like these. The change will continue to be profound as advanced analytics, artificial intelligence, robotics, cloud computing, quantum computing, the Internet of Things, and blockchain technologies transform data architectures, supply chains, labor allocations, and the very products and services demanded by consumers that make the whole wheel spin.

The beginning of the journey is to simply understand the external macrotrends that profoundly affect the company and its future. Draw out those variables that will affect your company, including their likely scale and dimension, influence on your market and competitive set, and pacing. These variables will inform your prognostications for what will happen and when.

Direct Implication (Stage 2)

This next stage involves decoding, transcribing, and integrating – a process I'll simply refer to as cross-correlating—the likely effect of these identified variables to the company's present and future market offerings. Now assess the company's corresponding ability to effectively monetize the financial value of these market offerings going forward.

P&L Design (Stage 3)

The third stage of this methodology involves cross-correlating the macrotrends (stage 1) and their direct implications on the company (stage 2) with its forecasted P&L. We are translating what began as something ethereal, visionary, bold, or different down into actual numbers. It is the process of transitioning ideas, concepts, and, quite frankly, the judgments and opinions of the executives, experts, and advisers into quantitatively expressed data elements. From here we can begin to see prospective trend lines and patterns. It gives us an understanding of what could become, sometimes with a fairly high level of probability, while at other times feeling like a Rorschach splat open to widely divergent perceptions and interpretations by those gathered around the table. Either way, there is tremendous value to the method. We are beginning to discover those deeper codes that can unlock the exponential financial value harbored within.

More specifically, and most obviously, this stage of the method reveals the likely implications to the go-forward P&L, providing us with visibility into prospective

revenue growth;

operational efficiencies from new organizational structures, workflows, and methods of leveraging assets;

functional capabilities or deficits within our organization;

investment priorities going forward;

effect on our people—including possessing a cadre with the mind-set necessary to unlock the potential value promised; and

necessity to create new or revised value chains around the company. Very often it will become clear that we need a new "web" of contracts around the company. That is, we need a series of new or revised relationships with those third parties necessary to unlock the exponential financial value envisioned. These contracts will necessarily embrace a new approach, scope, and structure.

This is a highly revelatory process. It is yielding insights not only to the quantitative dimensions of the challenge ahead. It is doing something else. Of more profound significance to

The Craft, we are bringing to the forefront of the analysis the ways in which the various actors participate in the process. We are decoding not only how the variables that will underpin corporate growth, innovation, and transformation move but also more fundamentally why they move the way they do. This is where the deeper codes will be found.

Here's what it looks like. In the gray conference room, the forecasts and trend lines will be projected onto the screen for all to see. Each person will study the numbers and patterns with intensity. It is supposed to be an intellectual, analytical process. It often becomes judgmental and emotional. Some comments and questions are spoken. Many more are not. Each individual peering at the screen is encountering a particularly effective stimulus that in turn triggers individualized perceptions. These perceptions influence the reactions that ensue. Some will be consciously developed and purposeful. Many others percolate up from the subconscious. They can range broadly—for example, from how the viewer perceives the value of the present exercise to their stark opinion of the others in this room. In many cases, the exercise will trigger an even deeper set of patterning pertaining to their very self-identity. They are asking,

"Can this be true?"

"I don't believe this will play out like this."

"Is this what I am signing up for? Can I do this?"

It is all extremely relevant to *The Craft*. Your read is deepening, and if done well, your probability of unlocking exponential financial value in the future is now arcing upward.

A Sidenote on Cross-Correlating

The process of cross-correlating the diverse data sets—including those elements that are revealing themselves both above the waterline and bubbling up from below—is integral to this methodology.

Each stage of the method is distinct. However, it must integrate with the multidimensional whole. This is how we come to see things, attain new insights, and develop a depth of understandings that others cannot. It is how we pull back the shrouds and find the deeper truth—sometimes even the secret truth—that lies within. To do this, at each stage, we are cross-correlating what is known from other stages back into the present stage of our journey, creating a compounding body of knowledge that becomes more illuminating.

One of the most fundamental challenges for companies navigating through more complex dynamics and more complicated organizational structures, while continuing to

Illustration 2

Unlock Exponential Financial Value
Outcome

Reallocation of Rewards, Risks, and Responsibilities
Stage 6

Beliefs, Values, Attitudes, and Motivations
Stage 5

Cross-Correlating

Macrotrends
Stage 1

Direct Implication
Stage 2

P&L Design
Stage 3

New Ecosystems, Networks, Supply Chains, and Relationships
Stage 4

move at the exponentially faster pace of change experienced today, is that we lose sight of the integrated whole. It is a natural consequence of siloed organizations; the reliance on professionals with singular, unaligned areas of expertise; and a managerial interest in reducing the "noise" by keeping people within their respective running lanes. When we work with only the macrotrends (stage 1), their direct implication on the company (stage 2), and how it affects the P&L (stage 3), in reality we are working from a limited body of knowledge. It is where most companies stop. It is what they have always done. It is what they are told to do. They believe it is good enough.

Not anymore. There is more that we must mine. To not only survive the pace of change but also to actually thrive because of it, you have to go deeper. Rather than be fearful of or threatened by change conditions, there is the opportunity to capitalize on them. You just have to know where to look, what you are looking for, and what to do with it when you discover it.

The Craft relies on cross-pollination; cross-sharing; reaching across the many individualized domains to extract wisdom, insight, and commitment; and then integrating this understanding across the full span of the global macrotrends (stage 1), all the way down into the behavioral patterns and predispositions of those who will influence or determine the path of the company going forward (which will be discussed in the forthcoming stages 4 through 6).

To realize the benefit of this multidomain, interdimensional, full-stack methodology, always cross-correlate the insights and understandings from one stage to each other. Unlike

Illustration 3

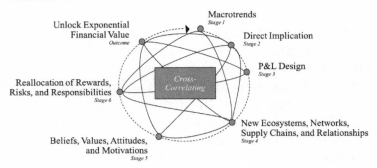

most companies, don't just tick off only the first three or four stages for developing your corporate strategy. In the accelerating environment, it is necessary to do all six. It is also necessary that it be overt and purposeful and not as an afterthought or incidental artifact of something larger. It is integral to unlocking the exponential financial value when the conditions of change, growth, innovation, disruption, disintermediation, transformation, adaptation, and positive evolution (that is, the force opposite to the one most companies will face over the coming decade that will lead to their stagnation, reduction, irrelevancy, and, ultimately, extinction) are upon us. Which they are.

New Ecosystems, Networks, Supply Chains, and Relationships (Stage 4)

The fourth stage involves cross-correlating the forecasted implications for the company's P&L going forward (stage 3) into the design of new ecosystems that will necessarily need to be created. This stage in the journey can be challenging. It requires creative, expansive, bold, and what sometimes even feels to some like reckless thinking. Pushing to the edge of discomfort is revelatory, often leading to breakthroughs by imposing interrupts into the stale and well-worn grooves of old thinking. It also improves the read on the actors at the table, testing their ability to contemplate the path forward while revealing many of their inner preferences.

This is why—to capture the power and potential value presented by new business models, rapidly advancing technologies, and other marketplace innovations—the organization will necessarily be forced to evolve—sometimes a little bit, often a lot. Consider the following internal implications to the company by evolving or creating the new ecosystems necessary to capture potentially exponential financial value creation.

First, new technologies often require substantial changes to workflows—in other words, who does what will change significantly.

Second, data architectures must often undergo radical upgrades in order to best serve the business, create new sources of value, integrate with a broader ecosystem of partners and vendors in the supply chain and delivery network, and integrate well with the systems, taxonomy, and syntax of a network of computing layers. In other words, the very nervous system of the company will necessarily need to change.

Third, the ways in which value is extracted from legacy capital assets and operations can shift momentously—the organs within the company must adapt, evolve, or in some cases be replaced with new or different ones to perform different functions now more imperative to the go-forward strategy.

Fourth, performance is delivered through broader ecosystems without regard to time zones, borders, languages, and cultures while the web of this performance network speeds exponentially faster with global communications networks, massive computing efficiencies, improved resource allocations, and the development of common practices, routines, and expectations across interdimensional, multicultural, and multidomain global networks. As a result, the brain of our living organism must send and receive signals faster, consume new information and recognize new patterns faster, develop new and more efficient routines faster, and integrate the signaling across the organization for broad consumption and understanding.

The logic of the organizational brain must be able to sever its reliance on legacy logical constructs and assumptions and be replaced with new constructs and assumptions better suited to the new paradigm. To illustrate, those companies with capex-heavy investments in transportation or real estate must respond to the new paradigm of ride sharing and home sharing, respectively. The fundamental tenets of the regulatory and licensing schemes on which the logical constructs they have relied for years have eroded quickly. If they are unable to swap out their prior logical constructs and assumptions with new ones, they lose significant financial value. Many will face the ultimate Darwinistic consequence of failing to adapt and evolve to new conditions—and simply no longer exist.

Or, to step back even further, in the several years leading up to the tech bubble of 2002, many commentators were making news by touting that the US economy had fundamentally changed due to the new technologies reshaping the world. They boldly announced that the old rules about economic cycles no longer applied and that we were truly entering into a new era of unassailable prosperity. Their boldness got them airtime. Their prognostications, however, proved false. The US economy tumbled, setting off a major reset across all sectors.

At this point in time, I was building new ventures for a global corporation that had just hit a narrow window for a successful IPO. We had ridden the technology boom up and rung the bell. Now we would be riding it down. The economy was not unassailable, nor was this newly minted public company. For years, the company had sold multimillion-dollar ERP systems to major corporations around the world. It was a high-dollar but basically cash-based business. Money in, money out. Not rocket science. Just big rockets. After the bust, the big customers didn't have the money for multimillion-dollar IT expenditures. Their businesses contracted, and ours would too. I spent the next several years building market offerings to reflect these new market realities—namely, these clients still needed lots of technology and the smart minds to put it in, but they needed a pricing structure, contractual model, and longer period to pay for it. I was building business models that would come to be the early precursors to what today is the ubiquitous SaaS (software as a service) delivery model.

At the time, fundamentally transitioning this business model was a tough sale, both internally and externally. The financial mechanics to implement this transition were used by other leading outsourcers, but they were novel to this organization. The approach necessitated shifting significant capital investments that historically were on the client's ledger onto my company's own ledger and then structuring a long-term contract to recover this investment, plus a cost of capital. The numbers worked. In fact, they worked very well, but only if we could fundamentally reconceptualize how we thought about the numbers and risk.

The transition also required the organization to shift how it approached performance and legal obligations. Instead of having expensive consultants fly in to client sites to do all the work of setting up complex systems based on Oracle, SAP, Siemens, or a host of other vertical market applications, and then at the successful conclusion of the project fly out and move on to the next client, this longer-term approach required the organization to maintain the system for years. In other words, they had to live with it, for better or for worse. They were assuming the risks associated with its performance. This was new territory. This was a new mind-set.

Finally, because of the shift from relatively short, wham-bam types of implementations to an encompassing managed services delivery model, the organization had to develop an entire ecosystem of new vendors around this practice, including network providers, security providers, data centers, call centers, financing entities, escrow companies, and a myriad of others. We were still in the business of baking cakes. The recipe, however, was very different.

This new way of developing, implementing, provisioning, and supporting major technology systems is now de rigueur. All technology companies strive to create strong recurring-revenue foundations under their own P&Ls while making their product offerings more easily consumable by their clients—including technologically, operationally, and financially. It was the right transition to make at the right time, both out of necessity and out of opportunity. Yet, internally, the senior executives in charge struggled to make the transition, even with a gun at their heads due to a constricting technology spend in the marketplace and a new set of public shareholders who wanted to see material progress quarter over quarter in terms of the financial performance of the company. Externally, the clients also struggled to make the change. They would repeatedly kick the can down the road, seeking more information, trying to ensure that they had vetted every new risk they could identify in this unfolding new world, debating new options and pathways, and, generally speaking, avoiding commitments for fear of getting it wrong.

Many of these entities no longer exist. They were big players at the time. But they couldn't manage through the evolutionary gauntlet brought on by a major shift in their environment. Darwin got them. After several hundred thousand miles on airplanes around the world working with clients and prospects to forge a path forward, and literally hundreds of iterative financial models, solution design sessions, presentations, demonstrations, pitches to CEOs and their executive team, deal negotiations, and ongoing performance updates, I slowly came to realize that the challenge wasn't a problem with the approach, models, pitches, or negotiations. It was about the more fundamental lens through which these CEOs and their executive teams—both internally and externally—viewed the world. Some could see into the future, envisioning a path forward and making the commitment to act on it. Many others could not.

Darwin got them too. Many times the greatest risk is not making the wrong decision but, instead, making no decision at all.

Beliefs, Values, Attitudes, and Motivations (Stage 5)

This is why you have to get into stage 5. Beliefs, values, attitudes, and motivations.

The macrotrends spawn new paradigms. The models change. The logic changes. The ways in which the whole ecosystem relates and behaves changes, often radically.

We now wade into the deeper codes at play—the motivations, expectations, standards, beliefs, values, preferences, and patterns of the individual actors on the stage.

This is where we must cross-correlate what it is that we are learning from below the waterline into the business going forward.

Most companies don't.

They go from the market analysis, financial modeling, operational planning, technology planning, marketing, and so forth, straight over to vetting and negotiating the relationships they believe are necessary going forward. They go from the early stages of the flow (stages 1 through 3) to the end of their journey (stage 4) because it is expedient, it is the path they have trod in the past, or it is what the management consultants, experts, advisers, and lawyers have told them naturally comes next in their journey. Sometimes it is the path they take simply because they don't know any other.

It is a mistake. This is the realm in which the potential for creating exponential financial value is—or is not—realized.

The failure to go below the waterline—decoding, transcribing, and integrating what is known about the underlying beliefs, values, motivations, biases, and preferences of the actors—leads to lost investments, lost time, and significant frustration with the slog their underinformed journey will inevitably be.

The failure to delve into this realm means, collectively speaking, trillions of dollars in potential value is left on the table. Literally. This staggering amount of lost value is due to

> failed or misdirected due diligence;

> sales pursuits that never go anywhere because of inarticulate selling propositions to poorly understood buyers;

> negotiations that blow up for a whole host of reasons— some of which are legal, operational, or financial— while others (if you scratch below the surface) are really due to how the parties to the negotiation came to the table with very different imprints for how they perceive, react, and think;

> contracts built to serve legacy, outdated business models being crammed down onto—and ill-suited to serve—emerging business models; or

> operational, technological, and delivery approaches mapped to the way business was done—rather than how it now should be done—in order to capture the

promised financial value.

Which leads us to where the secret codes lie.

The most challenging paradigm for companies to discover, design, and realize the promised potential value is wrapped in the riddle of navigating the potential new relationships, new ways of thinking and striving, and new mechanisms for providing value to one another. Cross-correlating this newness into the financial, operational, technological, reputational, and legal fabric of the business going forward vexes most.

It is the great mash-up.

Most companies do very poorly at the mash-up, even with a gun to their heads.

They cling to the rules, structures, and precedents of what they have known—desiring to protect legacy revenue streams, operational models, organizational structures, and people. Others just cannot conceive of a different path or stomach the tough decisions that necessarily come with turning the ship to face a different point in the distance.

The Craft is built on a fundamental reality—which is just as true for the large multinationals as it is for midmarket companies or early-stage innovators—about how corporate decisions are made. Ultimately, the most critical decisions are made by a small group of executives, or possibly even a single decision maker—depending on the governance model of the organization. Extending out from this core, of course, are the key influencers, advisers (accountants, experts, lawyers, bankers, and consultants), and overseers (boards, shareholders, debt holders, regulators, etc.) The universe affecting this decision is nonetheless quite small.

Given the reality of how the decisions are both influenced and made, the map will actually be quite small. Because of this, we are usually only dealing with a handful or two of people who truly determine what's next.

Given this limited cast of characters, it is both reasonable and imperative to

> understand how these distinct actors perceive, react, and think, both individually and as a group;

> decode their underlying beliefs, values, preferences, biases, triggers, and emotions; and

> cross-correlate these insights and understandings into the new ecosystems, networks, supply chains, and relationships necessary to successfully realize the exponential financial value promised.

The implication of this stage on the go-forward strategy is significant. More often than not, it will be determinative of your probability of success.

Several years ago, I began pursuing a deal with a midmarket company. They were entering into a period of significant investment for a product that had languished in their portfolio for nearly five years. They felt the market conditions were ripe for the push. They were committing to add $3 million per year in investment to expand their geographic footprint in the United States. The bulk of the investment would be in very traditional sales and marketing efforts. Their forecasts indicated that they could double the valuation on this product to around $50 million in two years if they were successful with the strategy. If they could ring this bell, they felt they were in a position to sell this branded product to one of the five big boys in this market segment and realize a significant return on investment for their private equity investors.

We worked with the team on their strategy and developed a way to further amplify its potential, enabling them to increase their geographic coverage from less than 50 percent of the United States to nearly 95 percent while significantly reducing their costs to achieve each incremental sale. If this approach were successful in establishing a truly national sales model for this product, it would put the company into a position of a targeted $100 million valuation. The approach—again, codeveloped with the client—was innovative, putting into motion a long-talked about path forward within the industry, now made real and tangible. It would, however, be one of the first attempts to deploy this approach in the US. There had been pockets of success with some incremental projects that were analogous to the proposed strategy. But there were as of yet no proven home runs. The company would be betting on a market innovation, tackling a paradigm that affected an entire industry, seeking to write the rules in their favor, and being rewarded handsomely if they were right. It is the promise made to all market innovators.

The bet was to add a $500,000 investment per annum to realize a prospective gain of $50 million in valuation within three years. They would be unlocking the value of the asset, big time, and potentially unlocking the value of an entire category of products across the US that they would steward. The investors who had been holding this languishing product for years would experience a jump in their return on investment from around fivefold to tenfold while putting themselves into position to replicate the approach with other products in a category that was languishing. In other words, the opportunity was not only for short-term financial gains but also to transition the very company from its position as a small player in a large industry to becoming one of the market innovators that championed the next five to ten years of growth. They could redefine what this company was and the value it would create for many, launching them all on an exponentially higher trajectory.

We met with the CFO several times over the course of codeveloping the approach. He understood it, the projected upside, and the associated risks of loss ($500,000). We pressed on. After six months of development, extensive consultations with all the senior executives and their expert advisers, and a final two-hour working session to make the go or no-go decision, he blinked. He couldn't pull the trigger on the $500,000 investment.

Over the span of these six months, a logical strategy was developed. The timing was right. The right players who were necessary to be successful were put into position along the value chain. The potential prize at the end—truly an exponential financial return on an asset that had languished for five years—was phenomenal. Everything above the waterline was a go. Until it wasn't. What killed the deal was something that percolated up from below the waterline—within a single individual at the table.

"I don't want to go first," he said.

He couldn't take the risk. He didn't want to be responsible for being wrong if the strategy underperformed.

The emotion of fear trumped opportunity.

Mapping the underlying beliefs, attitudes, values, and motivations of the individual actors at the table is critical to ensuring the probability of your success in unlocking exponential financial value. I've learned it the hard way.

Reallocate Rewards, Risks, and Responsibilities (Stage 6)

All companies must constantly enhance their competitiveness among legacy competitors and those emerging from new places, increase their resilience by managing the dynamic forces changing within their environment, and maximize their probability of successfully realizing exponential financial value. With the insights and understanding ascertained through *The Craft*, it is possible to do so.

If you have successfully reached this stage in your strategic development—including ensuring that the underlying beliefs, attitudes, values, and motivations of the actors responsible for its execution are aligned (stage 5)—then we reach stage 6: reallocating the rewards, risks, and responsibilities among the parties in the value chain or ecosystem.

The reallocation must be done proportionately, transparently, and equitably among all the parties within the company's evolved ecosystem. Most typically, this includes significant new players, each possessing differing mind-sets, expectations, standards, beliefs, preferences, and biases. They will need to be mashed together into new relational forms, new delivery models, new performance requirements, and new schemes for the financial exchange, all codified in new legal agreements.

The Craft moves us from the global macro to the financial and operational specific, all the way down into the micro, subtle, ethereal—that place where the deeper codes lie—enabling us to correlate the financial outcomes we seek with the beliefs, values, attitudes, motivations, and associated neurological, psychological, and emotional patterning of the actors who will make it so.

PART 2

METHOD

7

READ-FIRST

The Craft is a practical methodology. It reveals the dynamics that influence how value is truly created, including not only those dynamics transparently revealed by the actors—all the things we talk about at the big conferences and in our gray conference rooms—but also those that lurk below the waterline. It is these that must be drawn out and integrated into the design of our path forward.

Many corporate executives, lawyers, bankers, consultants, and experts walk into a room or come onto a call and immediately press forward with their objectives, agendas, and views. Most of the audience checks out quickly—glancing at their smartphones and thinking about lunch—already disengaged, unmotivated, inattentive, and unpersuaded. In contrast, *The Craft* begins with a read-first orientation. To do magic, you have to know where the audience is—in this moment. You have to read the room first. I know that what is about to unfold in this gray conference room will act as a powerful stimuli, provoking a series of reactions and responses. Each individual will react and respond in a different fashion, based on the unique patterning, biases, and beliefs they bring to the table. Some reactions and responses they can control. Others they cannot. I am the same. Their reactions will stimulate my own patterns, biases, and beliefs, provoking my own reactions and responses. This is all just the great soupy mix of people trying to find ways to relate, communicate, and move forward—in this case toward a common corporate objective. The difference is that we are now stirring the soup faster and faster, expecting the great mash-up to come together faster and faster. Usually it doesn't. It gets messy. It gets emotional. There is conflict. It plays out before us or under whispered breath later. Either way, we are left with less while those competitors—including those we know and those who emerge from new places with new ideas and new approaches—move ahead.

To facilitate the process moving faster and more successfully, I have found ways to increase the cadence of this inevitable mash-up of people. This method also helps transition what typically initiates as a fear-driven exercise—a natural product of how our brain processes any change condition in the environment—into a process where we are gleaning opportunities hidden away within the folds of this change. Know what clues and tells will be key with your audience for the purpose of assessing their perceptual state, reactions, and emotions in this moment.

Once assessed, you then can purposefully create the conditions that lead to the higest probability of success—for both the individual and the company. You are beginning the process of mapping what needs to take place above the waterline in terms of assessing the change conditions, whether they are a threat or an opportunity, with those dynamics that will play out below the waterline.

8

THE SKETCH

I've done them in conference rooms, hotel lobbies, restaurants, private residences, and airports—from San Francisco to Munich, Washington, DC, Dubai, Mexico City, Kiev, Akron, Tokyo, Singapore, and hundreds of locales in between. Sometimes more than a dozen people are there. Sometimes just one. After nearly three decades of doing it, despite the time zone, geography, culture, language, or imperative of the moment, I have distilled it down to one simple exercise. It is the next step in the process.

It works like this:

1. Draw a basic graph on a whiteboard or piece of paper.

2. Label the x-axis Time.

3. Label the y-axis Financial Value.

4. Write The Corporate Imperative across the top of

the chart as its title.

Illustration 4

THE CORPORATE IMPERATIVE

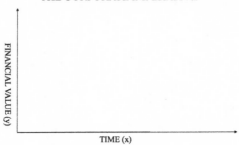

FINANCIAL VALUE (y)

TIME (x)

5.   Discuss among the group the values that should be assigned to the variable of time: How long will it take to achieve the outcome desired? Then discuss what the financial value achieved for the company in that time frame should be.

Note that sometimes the corporate imperative that draws us together in this moment will be easily defined against the two axes. There is a capital raise, for example, that must occur by a certain date (time) that must result in a certain amount of capital attained (financial value).

Or there is a tender process under way. The RFP sets forth the end date (time). The value of the potential sale will have a fair amount of certainty (financial value).

At other times, however, the corporate imperative may be known, but plotting it against the two axes of time and financial value will be difficult. Such corporate imperatives as making strategic investments, securing exits or spin-offs, managing disputes, navigating crises, pursuing policy agendas, moving in response to a changed condition in your market or by a competitor, and scaling a business up or scaling it down—all of which are critical to the company and may become one of the inflection points people will later point to, for better or for worse—can be difficult to plot on the graph. The conditions are vague, uncertain, or fluid. Or very often, no one can, has the desire to, or possesses the ability to place either a target financial value on the desired outcome or pin its achievement to a certain date (time).

Nonetheless, press on. This is critical, even in the face of frustrations. You are provoking revelations you will come to need. Some will emerge very subtly. Others will be glaring.

Plot the agreed values against the x-axis (time) and the y-axis (financial value), as shown in Illustration 5.

6. Mark the point on the graph where the two variables intersect, which should be toward the upper right corner of the chart. Label that point of intersection as the Optimal Value.

Illustration 5

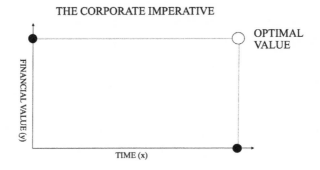

THE CORPORATE IMPERATIVE

7.   Draw a line from the zero point on the chart (the lower left corner of the chart) to the optimal value.

That's it.

Illustration 6

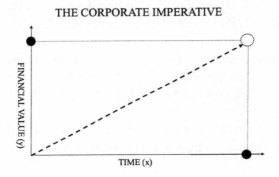

THE CORPORATE IMPERATIVE

9

THE DEBATE

A ctually, there is one final step to creating the sketch.

Simply close your eyes and imagine the debate that will ensue as the group negotiates the value for this corporate imperative against the two variables—financial value and time.

Not to overstate the importance of this, but often the corporate imperative being modeled with the sketch is the very event they will later point to and exclaim, "There, that was it!" For better or for worse.

Now imagine what you are looking for as you get your first read from the debate under way in the room.

The interpersonal dynamics.

The motivations of the individual actors.

What is and isn't being said.

Who engenders feelings of trust and why.

The probability of success in achieving the optimal value—that point in the future where you have successfully unlocked the target financial value for the company.

I have spent endless hours fueling this debate, coaxing and cajoling the actors to do more, go where they don't want to go, and think about things in ways that are challenging, frustrating, or what they would label impossible, radical, or even reckless. Because it tells us something. It shapes the ideas. More importantly, it reveals the deeper genesis of those ideas, how they bubble up, and how they come to develop texture and color. It reveals how the group behaves and the dynamics that work positively or negatively to engendering the development of a path forward. It reveals how the intellect, creativity, and emotions of the individuals gathered together meld to create an even more intelligent, more creative, more powerful collective brain. Or don't.

We are quickly entering a period of phenomenal change brought on by the ability of various technologies, including advanced automation, robotics, and artificial intelligence, to assume responsibility for an increasing portion of those tasks based on programmable logic and physical or cognitive routine. This will be a threat to many. For those who understand that within these conditions of change will also be the source of opportunity, they will realize that the capacity and methods to harness the creative, emotional, and empathic capabilities of individuals and teams working together—wading through the great soupy mix it inevitably will be—will be one of the most valuable resources to the future.

10

THE MIRROR

*Everything in this book can be used by you
or against you.*

This is your mirror. This is your lens.

It will reveal your potential.

It will determine your legacy.

11

COMMON WISDOM

We have the sketch. It will guide our path forward.

There is a problem, however.

There is no Sarbox disclosure for it. Perhaps there should be. It is a huge management risk that if known and understood might warrant disclosure. It just doesn't seem to be, or if it is, would be career suicide to admit.

The risk in this moment is that the path forward is defined by the same actors, doing the same thing, with an approach that is basically the same as what they've done before.

You can hear them now:

"This is a best practice."

"I've been doing this for twenty years."

"It worked before."

When you do the same thing over and over, there is an outcome that you are agreeing to—it is just part of the common wisdom:

You will have about the same probability of success as you did before.

It is a theoretical outcome, but it is generally agreed. In all likelihood, it will go unchallenged in your debates about the best path forward.

Unfortunately, it will be proven wrong.

Your competitors are moving faster, have better tools, have invested in better intelligence, and are using better analytics.

They know where you are entrenched, leveraged, stuck, lethargic, inexperienced, or naive, doing the same predictable thing time and time again.

They can anticipate your next move.

In the corporate world, when you do the same thing over and over, something else happens, statistically speaking:

Your probability of success goes down.

Sometimes a little. Sometimes a lot. Sometimes you don't even see it coming.

We can read you. It is not that hard. It will be used to your disadvantage.

12

EVERYTHING THAT COMES NEXT

Now intensify the debate going on in the conference room to see what else can be provoked and revealed.

Beside the point labeled as the optimal value, write the agreed financial value in dollars (or your preferred currency).

Below the stated optimal value, make a list of everything that comes next for the company once this point is successfully achieved.

Define that something greater:

1.   What doors now open for the company?

2.   What can the company now do?

3.   Who will now want to be a part of the company's journey from this point forward?

Illustration 7

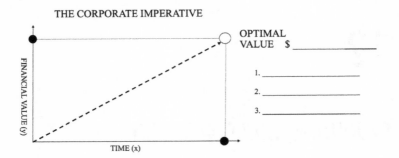

THE CORPORATE IMPERATIVE

The optimal value is not the destination. It is merely a benchmark of progress along our journey.

Metaphorically, the optimal value represents that door in the darkened night in our immediate future through which—once opened—leads to something even greater for the company on the other side.

These questions should provoke brilliant debate. Observe the reactions unfolding in the room. Build out your read.

See who opens up as well as who grows quiet.

Listen for fissures and friction and for those motivations, opinions, and fears that are both spoken and unspoken.

The actors around the table will begin to reveal themselves, and archetypes can help shorthand how each respectively contributes to the collective intelligence moving forward. You will discover the sleepers, doers, farmers, hunters, truth tellers, BS artists, resistors, skeptics, and seers.

Begin tapping into the imagined potential of what could actually become, the map for getting there, and who can contribute to making it so.

13

THE VECTOR

The vector is the trajectory between the starting point on our graph and the optimal value. It is the line moving from the lower left to the upper right. The challenge for

Illustration 8

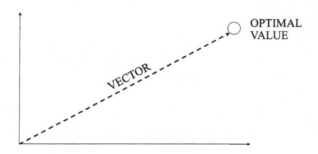

The vector never actually moves this way.

It will never be a straight line. It will never even have a gentle curve to it.

Instead, the actual vector will ebb and flow. It will be winding. At times it will feel like you are on a roller coaster. At others it will feel like a never-ending slog.

Illustration 9

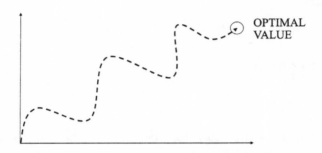

At some moments it will feel as though the potential financial value of this initiative could explode beyond your dreams. At others it will feel like the value that will be created will be little to nothing—all the toil and effort will likely be for naught.

The actual vector will be defined by the events, actors, and challenges encountered along the path. It is a bubbly mix—often unpredictable and always challenging—and, consequently, it behaves like a living beast, ever changing, with its own physio-neuro-psycho-emotional dynamics at play.

Like all living things, there are some things you will be able to see and touch and know. Others—more subtly, imperceptibly, unconsciously, or that are down within the codes of the DNA of this living beast—will be at work below the waterline. These forces will define the behaviors and outcomes of the inflection points. They are powerful. In fact, quite simply, they will determine whether you succeed.

Each of the inflection points you will encounter along the vector represents an opportunity for the corporate imperative to go off the rails.

The deal stalls.

The dispute develops new wrinkles.

The regulatory policy shifts.

The financing is delayed.

Someone pulls out.

Another does not perform.

Illustration 10

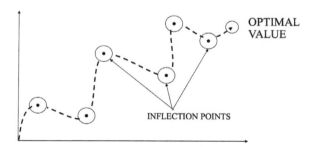

When you have seen these moments—which we all have—it often had little to do with contracts or pricing or the words spoken. More often the real reason is because

management just didn't get it,

they moved too slow,

they were paralyzed, or

their egos got in the way.

14

THE CALCULATIONS

The challenges for most companies is that they spend significantly to calculate their projected vector. They have their own rocket scientists—the finance guy, the marketing guru, the ops gal, the project manager. Most of their calculations will be right. They will, however, be based on their own math.

The actual vector will often prove their math wrong. This is frustrating. It is expensive. From where you stand, it looks like the same people doing the same thing over and over again, with the same probability of success—but usually lower.

The problem is rooted in the fact that their calculations never include all the variables that affect the actual vector—those that will cause it to deviate substantially from the projection.

This is inevitably because the truly determinative variables of our success are not necessarily quantitative. Yet they always affect the time. They always affect the financial value.

With *The Craft*, they will become part of your calculations of the determinative variables.

15

ASYMMETRIC ADVANTAGE

The never-ending quest of corporate leaders is to create competitive advantage in the market.

In today's world, it is usually done by hiring the best people and advisers possible; optimizing business models; building new supply chains that disintermediate inefficient players and functions; investing in sophisticated data analytics and technology innovations that can transform markets; and creating full ecosystems around their businesses with strong relationships that are intelligent, responsive, and nimble.

There is another way to create competitive advantage.

By reading a different set of clues.

By looking for other patterns.

By unlocking the passageway in the darkened night with a different set of codes.

These are the ways to create asymmetric advantage in favor of the beholder.

16

EXPOSE THE DETERMINANTS

The sketch on the whiteboard, and the ensuing debate, will reveal many things we can objectively discuss, including such variables in the calculations as financial projections; consumer uptake; pricing; or time to market, time to scale up, or time to scale down.

The sketch does something else.

It quickly exposes the variables lurking below the waterline, including

the creativity of the team;

their openness to new ideas and influences;

whether they have an appetite for, or aversion to, risk;

their emotional predisposition, including expressions of frustration, anger, or fear;

how information is disclosed, how it flows, and who influences its interpretation; and

how power is being used.

This latter set of variables is some of the most determinative to whether the optimal value will be achieved. Metaphorically, I can now place a bet in the horse race that is forthcoming. I know whether this company is a horse that will go off as a two to one favorite or if it is a one hundred to one long shot. It is a calculation of the probability of risk in reaching the goal as well as the reward that will be realized if successful.

These variables, once revealed, do even more:

> *They tell me whether the optimal value can*
> *be pushed even higher.*

Usually it can.

The path to even greater financial potential is being unlocked.

17

THE CRAFT

Along the vector, numerous inflection points will be encountered. There are three truths to all such inflection points.

First, each possesses a unique set of probabilities. Depending on how each inflection point will be encountered and managed, individual probabilities can be attached to each alternative outcome, including, for example,

going off the rails;

slowing, stalling, or succumbing to inertia;

moving too fast;

giving away power;

leaving money on the table;

being surprised, blindsided, or outmaneuvered;

limiting strategic options or future value; or

failing to achieve new insights and breakthroughs.

These potential outcomes for each inflection point portend quite different possible vectors for the corporate imperative— with radically different contributions and deductions from the financial value that ultimately can be created.

The second truth is that the behavior of each inflection point is dependent on three primary variables and their cross-correlations.

These variables and their cross-correlations, collectively, are the algorithm.

Illustration 11

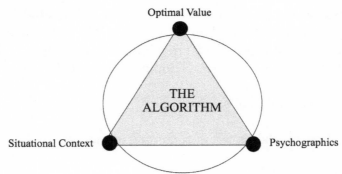

The dependent variable in the algorithm is *optimal value*, which we have already established through the process of the sketch. The optimal value reflects—first and foremost— the targeted financial value to be realized from this corporate imperative. The company's performance—and those who lead it—will ultimately be judged by whether the optimal value is achieved.

The next variable in the algorithm is *situational context*. The situational context is dependent on the externalities that are affecting the behavior of the inflection point and may either be naturally occurring or purposely invoked.

The final variable in the algorithm is *psychographics*, which pertains to the behavior within the inflection point resultant from the beliefs, values, attitudes, patterns, and other related cognitive, emotional, and even physiological attributes of the actors engaged within the drama of a unique inflection point. These psychographic-related elements may also be naturally occurring or purposely provoked.

Optimal value is achieved as a direct product of understanding, managing, and even provoking the cross-correlations between the variables and then optimizing their behavior.

There is an extremely high degree of correlation among these three variables—that is, the influence and behavior of each variable both drives, and is in direct response to, the influence and behavior of the other variables. Therefore, it is the operating mechanisms within each variable that we seek to decode in order to optimize the path toward the optimal value—and certainly mitigate any of the adverse behaviors and influences we ordinarily witness.

The third truth is that mastering the understanding and integration of these correlations of optimal value, situational context, and psychographics within the algorithm is *The Craft*.

These correlations will determine

> which new doors of opportunity open for your company;

> how disputes will be overcome;

> how impasses are resolved;

> whether negotiations get back online;

> the size and future value of sales that are closed; and

> the nature and quality of the relationships your company possesses with its employees, investors, partners, suppliers, vendors, competitors, and opponents.

The algorithm will determine whether you achieve optimal value and

> whether your vector ascends more quickly or higher or instead slows, flattens, or falters;

> the sustainability of the vector over a longer period of time; and

> what new financial or strategic potential emerges for your company after achieving your optimal value.

The Craft is the integration of these multiple domains and dimensions into a singular method that creates exponential financial value for your company.

18

GLINT OF GOLD

Within the inflection points—as the situational context and psychographic dimensions are shifting, either naturally or due to provocation, management, and optimization—there are certainly risks.

But this is also where we will find the glint of gold.

Inflection points are gateway experiences, creating the opportunity for passage to something greater on the other side.

It is where the rules change.

Normal hierarchies are challenged.

Common wisdom is turned on its head.

Traditional paths are ignored.

Old calculations lead to dead ends and money is left on

the table.

Those who are entrenched in a static environment or who behave predictably can be thrown into conditions less familiar, more fluid, and less controlled.

This is our opportunity.

19

PRINCIPLES

Your probability of success increases exponentially by mastering how to decode and navigate the conditions and cross-correlations within each unique inflection point.

Know the following:

First, each inflection point is like a new down in an American football game.

Every down—or inflection point—represents a unique situational context. This, then, drives the corresponding philosophy, scheme, play, and individual players necessary to successfully achieve the objective of this down in the overall arc of the game.

As you vector into each inflection point, you can improve the intrinsic probabilities of success but only if you play the down well in that unique moment. Naturally, the probabilities decrease if you don't.

Second, what is at play in the behavior of each inflection point includes not only that which we can commonly see, hear, and know above the waterline—for example, the behavior of the financial numbers, the words on the announcement, the published actions by the regulator, and so on—but also what is occurring below the waterline.

This includes the behavior of those dimensions we cannot commonly see, hear, and know, including the biases, patterns, and preferences we each, individually and collectively, bring to the table.

For example, drawing from my own personal experience, it is important to know early if the CFO who desires creating the highest value exit possible for his private equity investors truly has the ability to embrace the bold plan for achieving it or if he will be hemmed in by the fear of potentially being wrong. It is important to know if the CEO of a $100 million midmarket company has the ability to negotiate with its major shareholders through a dispute or if he will succumb to being the weaker in a power-based relationship, letting the enterprise decline over the course of a slow, unresolved grind. It is important to know if the CEO who took over a multinational financial institution that had financially flatlined had the deeper conviction, character, and belief system to lead it through the many inflection points he would inevitably encounter along the growth path forward. He did, and the bank quadrupled its market cap within ten years.

These attributes are derivative of the logical constructs, worldviews, filters, and emotional triggers that function more deeply within each of the actors involved in the drama of the respective inflection point. Only the well trained can know, understand, decode, and recode these deeper and subtler dimensions. Being able to navigate well all that is transpiring above the waterline, as well as that operating below, is what increases the probability of success within the inflection point. It also enables you to successfully continue—efficiently and powerfully—your journey toward the optimal value.

Third, the probable inflection points can be identified in advance with a relatively high level of probability.

Really.

They then can be decoded, pre-scripted, and planned. Creating anticipatory advantage increases your probability of success—you see what it is coming before it happens and before others can perceive, react, and respond.

You are a step ahead.

Fourth, because the inflection points can be anticipated, we know how to devolve our read—gleaning the quick clues that inform our decisions and actions as we come into the situation and as it continuously evolves.

Quick reads and pre-scripted actions, particularly in the corporate environment, are immensely valuable to your probability of success.

Speed kills.

Fifth, understanding the inflection points helps reduce internal drag.

In pursuing complex, high-value corporate initiatives, there will always be the internal dissidents, detractors, short sellers, and risk averse whose hair-trigger amygdala is poised to issue the flight command. Their sensitivities are often measured by the distance between the actual vector and the projected vector they saw on the screen or in the deck before the launch. The greater the gap, the louder their cries. It is a drag on the organization.

By understanding the likely inflection points, anticipating them, and preparing for them in a rational and transparent manner in advance, the organizational focus and energy can be applied toward successfully navigating through the inflection points and achieving the optimal value.

Sixth, understanding the realities of the inflection points, and being able to craft a game plan that will successfully navigate through their conditions and the cross-correlations within the algorithm, creates asymmetric advantage for your company.

In other words, the conditions of the inflection points—the uncertainties, the drama, the noise, the confusion, and the pressure—will most probably have a predictably adverse effect on those who fail to understand and prepare for the inflection point. This is your competition—including those opponents who seek to impede your ability to achieve your optimal value. It challenges their cognitive, emotional, and physiological responses, often rendering them less able to see the path forward, operating from a reactive instead of a proactive state, and consuming energy to make sense of the shifting stimuli about them.

This asymmetric advantage is yours.

Seventh, because you possess the secret codes and method of *The Craft*—and are able to move faster, more nimbly, more aware, more insightfully, and more effectively—you will come to purposely seek out these inflection points.

Those with the skills and abilities, a game plan, and a team conditioned to manage progress through the actual vector by capitalizing on those opportunities where there is change, confusion, intensity, and conflict instead of running from them—including within each inflection point that emerges—gain separation from their competitors and opponents.

This separation creates financial value.

Financial value creates legacies.

20

PURPOSEFUL PREPARATION

This is a complex game. It is not for the naive, unwitting, or unaware.

Those who win at this game are masters of their crafts.

Masters do not just happen. They prepare for their moments.

They learn to anticipate well, finding clues that give them a half-step advantage when they need it.

They practice both the art and the science.

They have a game plan.

They know the philosophy. They can feel the rhythm within the moment.

They then peak. It will define their legacies.

PART 3

PROVOCATION

21

SUNLIGHT

The structures and techniques of *The Craft* have originated in extreme experiences. Extremes act as sunlight—exposing what is already there but which we otherwise could not see. It is how we reveal the deeper codes that truly affect outcomes.

This body of insights and learnings has been gleaned from such experiences as working with the CEOs of some of the largest corporations in the world, as well as the presidents of nations, technology innovators, investors, bankers, hackers, spies, and, quite frankly, some flat-out corporate scoundrels, all acting when the situational context surrounding them had grown most intense, chaotic, and confusing—those moments when they were pressured to ask, "What next?"

It has included working on corporate due diligence, M&A transactions, financings, corporate spinouts, reorganizations, high-dollar enterprise sales, international tenders, auctions, reputational campaigns, writing national laws, implementing internationally agreed-upon policies, corporate crises, regulatory investigations, criminal investigations, international disputes, and a myriad of other situations that had the potential to define everything that came next for the company and its executives depending on the outcome—for better or for worse.

It has come from knitting together the network of actors to create ecosystems that derive new financial value from new business models, new technology innovations, new policies, and new creative breakthroughs.

It has always become most revealing of the truth as the intensity of the moment ratcheted higher and higher—the sunlight growing brighter—because

the value of the deal was stepping up or falling away;

cash flows were depleting quickly;

the feeling of being leveraged grew heavier;

the options forward were diminishing;

the curated intangibles of a person's identity—including their political power, their reputation, or their legacy—were threatened; or

the actors in the unfolding drama moved in, moved out, played games, sought advantage, and revealed who they really were, what they really wanted, and what they could or could not really do.

This has been the sandbox for decoding and compiling *The Craft*—witnessing those who rose to the moment—and those who did not.

It is important to note that for those who underperformed or failed, it rarely had anything to do with intellect or intent. Instead, it most often had to do with their lack of insights and preparation for the fluid but predictable dynamics that most certainly come into play when the inflection points grow most intense. It did have to do with something deeper— including their own perceptions, reactions, and thoughts in the moments like these.

22

FINDING THE NERVE

I will admit to the thrill of working at the edge—those extreme experiences where the nerve is exposed—and the events, actors, and stimuli are all in a jumble.

The nerve becomes raw and exposed, and the truth comes to reveal itself—with no pretense, no time to develop a careful narrative, and no gatekeepers to protect what they would otherwise like to keep secret.

These are the types of experiences that reveal not only what we think but also how we think—or, in certain contexts, don't think at all.

These are the experiences that turn not on what it is that we say but instead reveal what we truly believe.

These are the experiences that reach down into those places where we have little conscious control—revealing the patterns, triggers, and emotions that percolate up not only to influence our experience but also, in many cases, to determine it.

This is where the deeper codes lie—beliefs, attitudes, values, and motivations.

These are the deeper codes that determine outcomes.

Once they are revealed, we can map the path to creating exponential financial value for our corporate imperatives—purposefully and consciously.

We determine our outcomes. We reveal the truth of what can be created. We define who we are.

23

REACTIONS

To navigate toward the crack of light where exponential financial value is created, the territory must be mapped. The territory ahead is complex, challenging, likely even treacherous. The maps most use have already led to dead ends, stalemates, clashes, disappointment, lost time, lost advantage, and lost money.

Something is missing.

Something elusive, ethereal, and hard to describe.

Something that is coy, preferring to lurk in the shadows.

Something subtle but pervasive and powerful.

What is coveted in gray conference rooms by strangers who have only hope is a map that charts a new path.

To do so, that something elusive, ethereal, and hard to describe must be coaxed out and revealed.

Various stimuli with *The Craft* are used. The sketch is one such stimulus. There are more.

These stimuli provoke reactions. The reactions then reveal the tripwires built into the conditioning and the patterns that lie below the waterline.

Once tripped, they set in motion the thoughts, words, and actions of the actors—all of which initiate before the person consciously thinks. The carefully conceived scripts, prepared narratives, and beautiful packaging fall away. The truth— once shrouded—is now revealed.

The Craft depends on provoking the reactions that reveal how the actors truly perceive.

What do they see?

What do they hear?

What are they willing to contemplate and conceive?

Through this, we are revealing the secret codes necessary to understand what they believe.

Then, once I know what they believe, I can know

what they expect,

what they hope, and

what they fear.

The beliefs do something else. They heighten or dull the

perceptual senses. In doing so, the beliefs and perceptions complete a self-reinforcing circle—believing only that which we perceive; perceiving only that which we believe. The very core of whether someone can envision, believe in, and work toward the optimal value is then revealed—their beliefs and perceptions may simply be unable to conceive of the potential.

Through *The Craft*, we are discovering the roots of what it is that causes some individuals to open up while others close down. We can identify what it is that causes some to fight while others determine to retreat, create, or destroy. We can see what conditions cause some to become less while provoking others to become more. We know those words, visual cues, logical sequences, and emotions that will resonate, provoking new ideas, meaningful action, and mutual agreement—and those that will repel or divide.

The Craft enables us to identify those actors who can find new ways of envisioning the path forward, together. We are able to find ways to break the self-reinforcing patterns of beliefs and perceptions and the traps of returning to circular debates, intractable arguments, and resorting to doing the same thing over and over rather than better and better. As a result, we are literally able to provoke the neurology to shift from lower-order fight-or-flight nonthinking—or, alternatively, zero-sum, winner-take-all thinking—and move into higher-order neurological patterns that draw from the realms of the quantum brain to spark creativity, inspire trust and goodwill, and achieve breakthroughs.

We integrate this understanding into the practical realities of running a business, including creating the necessary operational structures and day-to-day work plans, drafting the actual terms and conditions, and finding ways to allocate risks and rewards—fairly, equitably, and transparently—among ourselves and those who seek to be a part of our journey ahead.

We are then positioned to achieve optimal value, derived from a myriad of potential sources, including growing revenues, achieving greater efficiencies, resolving conflicts, launching new strategies, reorganizing the company, or revising our existing (or building new) ecosystems around us—with better, stronger partners, suppliers, vendors, advisers, experts, financiers, and others.

The map is revealing itself, simply as the conditions and cross-correlations operating within the algorithm are observed—and if necessary, purposefully provoked—to reveal the optimal path ahead.

24

THE PASSAGE

Every company has dynamics at work above the waterline and below.

We are working above the waterline when talking about markets, strategy, finance, technology, legal structures, investments, brand, identity, reputation, and the like. This is where most strategists, lawyers, investors, bankers, technologists, engineers, and consultants spend their time. Most corporate executives do too. It is a nice place to work. The common wisdom is that keeping everything in order above the waterline is how to make a nice living, live in a nice neighborhood, and have a nice vacation. There is truth in this—like all commonly held beliefs.

The problem is that it stops short of the full truth. Rarely is it in order.

Rarely is it where you win the game.

Knowing the dynamics at play below the waterline is where

you build the map that leads to the optimal value. It is then how you navigate to achieve optimal value—and then maybe even accomplish more. It is below the waterline where you find out what moves someone. It is where you find out where they will go

> if your deal is stuck—most likely it is something at work below the waterline where you'll discover why;
>
> when someone is stalling, sandbagging, or sowing discord, go look below the waterline;
>
> when you can't get folks to think outside the box— and you are desperate for a breakthrough—something below the waterline is holding them back; or
>
> when your CEO isn't able to make the play—like pitching the big deal, inspiring the employees, or playing defense when they should be playing offense— take a look at what is going on below the waterline.

There is a direct causal relationship between what you find below the waterline and your ability to achieve the stated optimal value.

Whenever I've been around something that has blown up—and there've been some doozies—the reason could be traced to a cause or dynamic below the waterline. It is usually something wired into the beliefs, attitudes, values, preferences, and triggers of the actor. Sometimes it was consciously experienced. More often it wasn't—it just happens because of something going on at a deeper level.

The remarkable thing is that it is the same for the work that has gone brilliantly—it was because of what was going on with dynamics at play below the waterline.

But this is precisely where we want to go. It is where we tap into tremendous creative resources that can imagine, conceive, and construct solutions for the future in a way that only the quantum human brain can.

The problem is that to get from above the waterline to below is tricky.

People guard it for a whole host of reasons.

Some of the reasons are rational. Others are not.

Some we are aware of or can be consciously perceived. Many others are not.

But it is below the waterline where they keep the good stuff.

To play at the highest level in the game, you have to get from above the waterline to below.

Passage is gained by using the algorithm.

The algorithm not only reveals the conditions and cross-correlations we seek to illuminate and understand but also determines

    whether passage will be granted,

    the depth of passage permitted,

    the nature and quality of the view we get,

the probability of getting our read and resulting action right, and

whether you will find the elusive crack of light to navigate through to create financial value.

25

STIMULI

Our perceptions, reactions, and thoughts are a product of the interaction between various stimuli we experience—both consciously and unconsciously. When stimulated, they activate against our patterns, preferences, biases, and triggers, which are in turn woven into the fabric of our cognitive, emotional, and physiological being—affecting us deeply. Ultimately, they determine what it is that we feel, think, and do—or what holds us back. This is a lot to unravel.

In fact, in the realities of managing complex corporations in frantically competitive environments moving at a faster and faster pace, it is usually all considered a jumble. It is something always at risk of teetering over only to unleash a hot mess—the great soupy mix. For most executives, we'd rather let it lie than risk tipping it over. The purpose of *The Craft*, however, is to tap into the greater potential that certainly and always lies within—while averting the hot mess that can bubble up from below the waterline. In fact, *The Craft* enables us to get a clean read,

decode the dynamics at play,

anticipate what will come next with a high degree of accuracy,

prepare well, and

execute into and through the inflection points that stand between where we are today and where we intend to be soon—the point of the optimal value.

When you stand on the sidelines, fearful of tipping over a hot mess, what happens is that within the critical inflection points you will inevitably face, you end up

winging it;

allowing those with the most seniority, most intrapersonal power, or biggest personalities in the room—and not necessarily the savviest as to the dynamics at play—to dictate what comes next; or

just doing it the way you did the last time.

When this becomes the default, you will have about the same probability of succeeding.

Actually, it will probably be less.

The Craft enables you to break down the true dynamics— rationally and transparently—understand their influence and importance, and then move forward to formulate a high-probability game plan.

The place to begin this methodology is by understanding and decoding the stimuli that are activating the actors within the anticipated inflection point. Many of the stimuli are a natural product of the conditions they face—including, for example,

> a revenue line that is eroding day by day;

> a share price that continues to decline;

> an explosion at a plant;

> a hacker who stole a couple of million identities out of your systems and is now selling them for five dollars a throw on the international black market; or

> any of the extraordinary events or conditions that intensify the noise, confusion, pressure, and intensity of the moment.

Other stimuli can be used as controlled agents—meaning they can be used to provoke a reaction or affect an intended outcome.

For example, in corporate negotiations, the situational context can be purposely intensified to increase the pressure on the other party, including, for example, by

> introducing new parties into the negotiation,

> shortening timelines, or

> starting simultaneous discussions with competitors.

Both natural and controlled stimuli like these change the situational context, which in turn stimulate the psychographics—and vice versa—revealing the interplay within the algorithm between how the parties perceive, react, and think and how the relationships are unfolding. By observing the reactions to both the natural and the controlled stimuli, we can anticipate what will come next in the patterns, biases, and preferences expressed and construct a high-probability path forward—working toward the ultimate goal of how best to create exponential financial value.

To some this may feel artificial. It may strike others as manipulative. Still others may not be able to reconcile this method with their own training, experiences, patterns, and preferences.

The Craft is—quite frankly—a method for finding and optimizing the path forward. In the corporate realm, the path necessarily involves creating, managing, and nurturing relationships with others—partners, vendors, employees, influencers, policy makers, investors, and a myriad of others. *The Craft* increases the probability of being able to successfully do so.

To create exponential financial value, these diverse groups or individuals—all of whom possess their own distinct logical patterns, beliefs, feelings, biases, and preferences—must come together in a relationship or network that establishes a vibrant ecosystem in service to a common objective.

Alignment or resonance among these actors is imperative. In fact, alignment or resonance will either fuel or impede the financial value you are able to create.

The process of finding this alignment and creating this resonance among diverse groups and individuals is, frankly speaking, a mystery to most corporate executives.

It is not their domain.

It was not their training.

It is often a messy quagmire they have largely avoided up to this point with some success and aren't about to step into it now.

For these executives, they will leave this mystery to some imperceptible alchemy or maybe just to the whim of chance.

Either way, the operative variables in the equation will remain hidden or unknown—and consequently cannot be included in the calculus for how to craft strategies for going forward—including those that promise even greater financial value and strategic potential.

As a result, many corporate imperatives that promise tremendous potential financial value to the company at least on paper will be stillborn. Others will gain early life, only to latercrash and burn at great expense and frustration. It is inevitably because they failed—either unwittingly or purposely—to anticipate the inflection points that will be encountered along the way toward achieving the optimal value.

The use of stimuli throughout the process of identifying, contemplating, socializing, negotiating, managing, nurturing, and optimizing this path toward the corporate imperative reduces the risk of stillbirth or crash-and-burn flameouts while significantly increasing the probability of success in achieving the optimal value.

26

EXTERNALITIES

Many corporate executives describe the predicament their companies face as the product of something happening "out there." A short seller or analyst. A competitor's move. A tax or regulatory change. A disgruntled debt holder. It is usually where our first conversation begins. It is true—there is something out there that is stimulating the conditions. It can be described. You and your stakeholders can point to a common enemy and say, "There is our problem." This is all logically sound. It is convenient.

But it is too simple. In fact, it may be a trap.

What is occurring above the waterline and below are never unrelated. They are integral to each other, including at both the company and the individual levels. Those who can see only what is outside of them but are unaware of how these stimuli are affecting how they individually perceive, react, and think—the fundamental functions that affect whether we are going to get that decision right in our most critical moment—are walking blind. They are likely taking us with them. This blindness leads to sluggish growth. Opportunities requiring quick reads and quick action are missed. The company's most valuable assets—many times the very individuals who are most creative, intuitive and empathic—move on, leaving the company depleted, unable to see, feel, and capitalize on those market dynamics where today's exponential financial value is being unlocked. They cannot sense the quickly shifting consumer preferences. They miss the arc on shifting generational, social, and technological trends. They are unable to compose new value chains that are more effective and disintermediate the old ones. They are unable to craft new ways of monetizing the value they create.

27

RESONATE OR REPEL

As a practical matter, for CEOs and corporate executives navigating their companies' trajectories forward, there is a constant process of looking for new partners, new vendors, new clients, and new employees. The strategists, financiers, lawyers, and advisers will do their analyses rooted in financial models, market assessments, structural approaches, and identifying the key metrics that will shepherd the journey forward. They will make their recommendations. It will be logical.

Using the stimuli correctly tells the CEO and executives something else, however. Something more insightful and more powerful:

Whether the parties should come together—
and how.

By using the *The Craft* properly, in fact, the CEO will be informed as to the probability of success for this relationship,

the time that it will take to establish and maintain,

the likely debates and pitfalls that will be encountered along the way, and

the amount of trust and reliance that should or should not be placed on the other party.

Whether and how the parties should come together—all in service to achieving the optimal value—depends significantly on how those respective parties perceive, react, and think. They should come together only when they

understand and empathize with one another;

resonate with one another—meaning they share motivations, beliefs, and values pertaining to their prospective commercial relationship; and

are able to operationalize the pathways forward in a manner that delivers mutual gain.

If these ingredients are missing or cannot be co-created, then the relationship should not move forward. This is not a loss and should not be regretted.

In fact, when there is a rational basis for the repel—the push away—it is extremely valuable to the company, financially speaking. When the repel is developed—purposefully, rationally, and transparently—it averts losses, including to capital investments,

opportunities foregone,

time, and

competitive positioning.

The stimuli are used in *The Craft* to simply reveal what lies below the waterline—below the intellectual analyses and forecasts that are part of the ordinary course of business operating above the waterline. The stimuli reveal

the deeper worldviews, emotions, strengths, and flaws of those across from you;

the vendors in whom you want to build your future;

which employees are going to get the job done; and

whose advice you will rely on.

The stimuli will also reveal who will be standing at your side—and who won't—

when the pressure is on,

when the waters get choppy, and

who will continue to be aligned with you when you need them most.

A significant portion of my career has been spent putting together consortia in the technology, telecommunications, health-care, pharmaceutical, banking, and energy sectors. Sometimes the purpose is to knit together a group of companies that can collectively pursue a commercial opportunity together, in some form or fashion. In other instances, I have created the playing field on which bidders fight for the opportunity, including in the context of international tenders and auctions. In either case, this has been the working laboratory for witnessing how individuals, teams, and companies come together with their myriad of diverse personalities, motivations, biases, beliefs, and worldviews. Or don't because of them.

At the beginning of this experience in the working laboratory, I would pound together these diverse parties out of sheer force of will. It was a simple, naive worldview that ran along the following lines: We were in a competition. The prize was at the top of the next hill. We would charge that hill regardless of what it takes to capture the prize. There would be casualties and losses along the way. We sometimes would reach the top of the hill. Often we didn't even reach the base.

Over time my perspective seasoned. I became better attuned to the real dynamics at play. There were still hills with prizes atop. But these are challenging, expensive, complex, and fatiguing journeys. The toll can be significant. Therefore, I'll march only with those who can be aligned. The reason is because the probability of success is low when the diverse players in a consortia, value chain, or commercial ecosystem are unaligned. There is too much friction. Too much posturing. Too much mistrust. Too much fighting. It is a drag on energy, time and resources. It hurts our ability to fight the battle "out there". Conversely, the potential for victory is high when there is alignment at the level of the deeper codes at play. In fact, it is the competitive advantage. Over time I came to realize that the greatest source of power in getting to the top of the hill was hidden within the deeper codes of those who would journey together. It was necessary to look for them, understand them, and know what to do with them. This is how you ascend the hill and capture the prize.

28

TIME

To begin revealing the deeper codes, the first stimulus is time. The influence of time strongly reveals the behavior of the cross-correlations between the situational context and the psychographic dimensions within the algorithm. How time affects or influences the perceptions, reactions, and thoughts of the actors can be extremely powerful in revealing the deeper codes affecting the behavior of the inflection point, the course of the actual vector, and, ultimately, whether optimal value can be achieved.

As a stimulus, time is sometimes obvious. The deadline for a tender submission. A reporter's deadline. Corporate announcements released after the closing bell. Press releases issued late on Friday evening. Regulatory filing deadlines. A cash call. A sale that has to close by the last day of the quarter to be recorded on the books.

At other times, it is subtler. The rhythm and cadence of deal negotiations. When to communicate with your own team as the business changes, evolves, or is reorganized. The pace of our campaigns to develop relationships, partners, collaborators, and competitors.

It is a determinant that reveals strengths we want to build on, fundamental vulnerabilities and weaknesses we seek to avoid, and the character and motivation of those involved.

Speeding or slowing the clock adds intensity and pressure to the situation, revealing

> tolerances for risk and uncertainty;

> underlying intellectual patterns—for example, what card is played next when someone feels rushed, pressured, missing out, or at risk of losing options forward;

> emotional reactions; and

> where financial value can be created—such as higher prices when selling or cheaper prices when buying.

Time is a powerful stimulus when activated either by accelerating it or slowing it for purposes of

> decoding the underlying logical constructs assumed by the parties as well as their worldviews, values, beliefs, and emotions;

> raising the level of disclosures and transparency; and

> forcing self-committed errors.

29

OVERLOAD

We all are slower and more unsteady at processing information when we encounter new situations.

When those new situations are layered with confusion, noise, pressure, and lots of money, the processing time gets longer and our probability of making a mistake is higher.

What is happening is that our perceptual sensors are lighting up.

We are getting tons of new and unfamiliar information.

Most likely, we haven't developed the neural patterning to process this information efficiently, which results in diminished performance and increased vulnerabilities because

> our brain considers the exercise to be a tax, as it is consuming a tremendous amount of energy, and therefore seeks to manage the load downward;

we don't yet trust the information, the patterns, or our read;

we are susceptible to the influence of others and haven't yet established the filters to determine what is best for our interests and what isn't; and

we are hesitant to act, shaky when we do, and prone to flubbing the call.

For those who own the responsibility to recommend, decide, and act in critical or high-stakes moments, these are poor psychographic and situational context conditions in which to operate.

It gets worse:

Cognitively, in moments like these, our cycle times are typically longer and therefore our probability of being right is lowered.

A psychological portal is opened to access our ego, self-identity, and emotional triggers.

Negative self-chatter will create an echo effect, amplifying the risk of getting it wrong.

Sophisticated competitors, negotiators, reporters, regulators, investigators, and others know this—which is why they create the situational context and stimulate those conditions with psychographic implications to open the playground.

30

CADENCE

The corporate game moves very fast now.

Many executives learned their craft at a time when things moved slower.

When they discover that they are moving slower than the situational context around them, they try to catch up.

They lunge forward and back.

They fixate on particular facts to the detriment of others.

They lose their fluidity of motion, becoming rigid in their thinking.

When they are on your team, they are hard to ease out of the way.

When they are on the other, they are easier to beat.

You can discover their reaction times and patterns and the corresponding influence these have on their cognitive and emotional responses by toggling the cadence of conversations, brainstorming sessions, negotiations, or other exchanges—cycling them either much faster or slower.

31

PREDICTABILITY

Many CEOs and corporate executives prefer working in carefully controlled environments where the patterns and routines are known and predictable. It is a natural comfort. In fact, it is a preference that roots down into neurological functioning. In short, the brain easily returns to the well-worn grooves of prior patterns and preferences. It is easier—less of a tax. This neurological pattern was likely further encoded through prior positive reinforcement. The executive did well in a previous experience and was rewarded. They would like to experience this situational context again, as there is a likelihood of a reward with repeated success.

The challenge, of course, is that the world is moving at an exponentially faster pace, with new bases of knowledge and understanding emerging that have a profound effect on the future of corporate strategies, operations, technologies, and business models. Those who are able to capitalize on these transformations quickly and efficiently rise to the top. Those who are entrenched—unable to react or respond well in highly fluid, chaotic, and ever-changing situational contexts—do not.

Understanding whether an actor—either individually or in their corporate form—has the ability to keep pace with the new models, bodies of knowledge, languages, concepts, and the innovative patterns unfolding in rapidly evolving situational contexts can be revealed by the stimulus of predictability.

The method for revealing whether this capacity is present in the executive and the corresponding level of development is to simply alter the logical flows of information, conversation, and dialogue to diversify its patterns. Shift from deductive structures to inductive, for example. Toggle the argumentation so that it appears unpredictable or even chaotic. Introduce new terms and concepts into well-established bodies of knowledge. Flip it, tease it, and all along, do it with purpose.

This will reveal several dimensions of value to your read that may not otherwise reveal itself unless purposely provoked, including

their ability to adapt quickly and effectively to alternative logical frameworks and sequential flows, including the presence of weak spots, blind spots, or latency;

the emotional responses that may be triggered by the expected patterns being modified, including indications of impatience, frustration, anger, cycling up, or cycling down; and

neurologically, whether the stimulus of information and

argumentation presented in new, different, or seemingly chaotic patterns cause this actor to open up—sparking the neurology of intellectual, high-executive, or creative functioning that underpins innovative or breakthrough thinking—or does it cause the actor to close down, eliciting at times even a fight-or-flight type response when the discomfort of not keeping up arises?

These are the insights we seek to know of prospective partners, vendors, suitors, employees, advisers, influencers, opponents, and others who will have an affect on our successful navigation through an ensuing inflection point.

32

CONTRAST

Strong, enduring relationships are built on trust. We use trust as a unit of measure, like degrees on a thermostat. We check the trust thermostat constantly—either consciously or unconsciously—just to see if we are running hot or cold in the moment. We do it

on the conference call to review monthly performance with a vendor, below the waterline of the conversation. We are asking, "Are they really telling me the truth?"

checking LinkedIn to see if you have mutual connections with a prospective new hire—if you both know the same person, this likely creates a predisposition of trust or distrust—by reference to your beliefs, feelings, and attitudes in relation to the common third party; or

when you are in the audience while the CEO is describing the performance to date and the strategy moving forward, you are asking, "Is she telling me the truth?"

Trust has texture and gradations. It is both spoken and felt. It is a concrete idea, and it roams in the ether. It is simple and it is complex. It is brazen and it is nuanced. Getting it right is hard. This has a myriad of relevant implications to *The Craft*.

First, we expect it to possess different qualities in different situational contexts. We are gauging the measure of trust we possess at a deeper level—assessing its quality and meaning with different actors under different situational contexts.

Second, every individual is programmed differently. Trust is something that operates cognitively, emotionally, physiologically, and energetically. Some people just project trust more easily than others. These are the patterns that lie below the waterline. It is not fair. It just is.

Third, we can use stimuli to more overtly test the qualities of trust we hold, understanding its texture, its gradations, and how it behaves in differing moments. These will become reference points for us, establishing patterns we may rely on. We will recall these patterns later, when we encounter new situations together, that test us, that intensify the experience, where the decisions and path forward could unfold in different ways based on our potential outcomes—for better or for worse. By using these stimuli to test dimensions of how trust behaves, we are then able to

better attach probabilities to the possible outcomes of our inflection points;

understand what conditions and patterns of the actors are likely to reduce our trust and reliance and thereby decrease our probability of success; and assess which conditions and patterns will increase the bond of trust and our reliance that their next action in a particular situational context will increase our probability of success.

Understanding these cross-correlations is very powerful. Rarely do we stimulate in a purposeful way to discover and grade the quality of trust. Instead, we do it indirectly, coyly, and, often, subconsciously. We talk around it, or when we do take it head-on, we do so in blunt, amateurish ways— for example, simply opining, "I don't trust him." More often we stumble into the question of trust, hitting a tripwire with some bumbling word or action during a conversation.

Much of my work has focused on asking people to assume risks – financially, legally, reputationally, egoically – associated with taking a more bold, creative, innovative path forward. We can all read the numbers in the spreadsheets, gauging the risk assumed relative to the probability of achieving the reward with such prospective paths. Very few, however, are willing to make the leap on the numbers alone. I have yet to meet a corporate executive, private equity investor, venture capitalist, or banker willing to make a bet on the quantitative dimensions of the leap toward building something new or better in order to unlock more financial value. Instead, they must come to hold that feeling of trust— in the person. Do they trust you to make the play? Trust is the qualitative intangible that counterbalances against their quantitative assessment of risk in the proposed leap across. If the level of trust they feel is less than their assessment of the financial risk, meaning the trust you project and they feel is less than the risk they take, they will not make the leap. Experienced institutional investors can get this read within the first ten minutes of a conversation. Maybe sooner. It is done extremely quickly in part because it is so central to the math of how they vet the hundreds of deals that pass across their desks each year. Here's the thing, though. Taking the leap toward something more bold, creative, and innovative requires that trust emanate out through the extended value chain. It is not a one-way exchange. If there is not a reciprocal feeling of trust with an institutional investor who may be a capital provider for the leap, then they should not be part of the leap. Why? It is too risky. It actually will hurt the probability of success. The relationship will fray quickly. Too much energy is spent trying to manage suspicions, backbiting, and whispers. At some point, there will be the inevitable bumble, and the delicate balance of trust will be broken. Thereafter, every decision from that point forward will labor through the feeling of mistrust. The tremendous amount of energy required to make the creative, innovative, and transformative leap to something greater out there is consumed managing the friction and tax in here. It consumes the organism from within. For those architecting new ecosystems around their businesses, establishing new value chains, negotiating new relationships, bringing new people into the mix with new ideas, different perspectives, and their own worldviews, preferences, and patterns, get beyond the conversations around pricing, terms, structures, and responsibility. Stimulate the patterns early to test for trust. Nurture it when it is present. Walk away when it isn't, even when you need their money, expertise, technology, or capability. The neurology that is necessary to create the optimal conditions for creativity, innovation, transformation, and other risk-taking in the individual and collective brain requires a foundation of trust among the parties. Expend the scarce resources of your time, energy, commitment, passion, and money with those you trust in your ecosystem. If absent, making the leap is not possible. It will just be a question then of how long it takes before it stagnates, regresses, or fails.

The stimulus of contrast can be used to observe a host of reactions that are important to getting your read, including, for example, the quality of trust. A two-step process is used. The first step is to establish parity with the other party. For example,

> in a conversation in which they are ultimately seeking agreement to a proposition (e.g., a sales pitch), indicate resonance with their ideas; or

> in a conversation in which they are seeking to establish superiority (e.g., as a negotiation), meet their power with power.

Observe the reactions.

Then, as the second step, shift to a contrast that is juxtaposed with or opposite to their current state. For example,

> if they are angry, then grow passive; or

> if they try to slow the pace, then rush it.

This simplified two-step approach of engagement simply shows how the actor responds to underlying patterns with which they are familiar and that are self-reinforcing, in contrast with those that provoke a reaction (which are best revealed by using a contrast—it triggers the pattern, bias, or objective so that it more readily appears). The revelation should represent a more true manifestation of their patterns, biases, or objectives.

The revelations will also be self-expressed, which is strongly encouraged to avoid the influence of your own biases and patterns adversely biasing a clean read.

The contrast technique works similarly—at least metaphorically—to a process described by Royce Alger, one of Dan Gable's greatest wrestlers, and a two-time NCAA champ and a World Cup silver medalist. Alger beat some of the greatest wrestlers in the world. He describes physically pushing in and out on the greats of wrestling to see how they responded, sensing their patterns and what their normal is. And then, when that pattern shifts, when they are out of their rhythm just a little bit—when the speed or movement of their reaction to his pressure shifts—he strikes. It is a small window, a small crack of light, but in that small moment, there is a valuable revelation. Perhaps even a world championship.

With this technique, we are creating a rhythm, a cadence, a system to establish parity or a state of what is considered normal. Then, when the contrast is used, we sense the reaction or opening, and we add it to our read. We are provoking an unthinking pattern to reveal itself—indicating the texture of an underlying emotional fabric, intellectual preference, or qualitative character we seek to reveal, such as trust—so that it can be added to our calculation of probabilities pertaining to the path forward.

33

SEMANTICS

I'm a liberal arts guy with a background in communications and several law degrees. There's a common thread that runs through a background like this: a fixation on what words mean—or, alternatively, how different people interpret the same words to mean different things.

More specifically, this fixation on semantics—which pertains to the use of language and words, including the underlying structures, meanings, and philosophical precepts associated with words, phrases, structures, and devices—has been in service to what I've needed to know in the real world, quickly and cleanly. Quite simply, I'm trying to identify what it is that gets people to move, resolve conflicts, do the deal, decide, stall, buy, sell, run, walk, fight, or stand down. I want to understand how the words—and structures used with those words—implicate movement.

As such, in the context of *The Craft*, various words, phrases, ideas, and concepts are used to test reactions; and

reveal biases, patterns, preferences, beliefs, values, motivations, and triggers.

This informs my read into the conditions and correlations affecting the algorithm, including

personal motivation, intention, and interpretation;

preferred logical structures (including the additive inferences, assumptions, and volumes of contextual information that are automatically appended to the discussion by individuals when certain words and phrases are invoked—virtual libraries of information and context that people drop into their frame of reference when contemplating ideas, proposals, offers, and so forth, once a word, idea, or phrase is invoked);

the ability to translate the words, ideas, and linguistic structures revealed in our proposals, offers, presentations, and other communications into the visualized, animated, living structures of corporate strategies, business plans, contracts, operational models, technology architectures, policy regimes, and the assorted other accoutrements of the corporate trade;

philosophical tendencies and structural preferences that reveal expectations of what a person believes should naturally come next in order to maintain consistency with the philosophy or structure—which can demonstrate a predisposition for what it is they may later agree to or reject;

emotional responses (e.g., anger, passion, invigoration, passivity, frustration, calmness, excitement, boredom) evoked by words, concepts, ideas, and structures; and

domain expertise, including the depth, diversity, fluidity, and ability to interweave multiple domains together to create new solutions.

The semantic stimuli are directly associated with the psychographic variable of the algorithm. The words literally stimulate alternative neurological patterns and reactions. This in turn can quickly activate shifts in the situational context. This is a good thing. It is very powerful. It can make the difference in whether we move forward or bog down.

Consider the following. We are in that gray conference room struggling to find the path forward. I may propose a path I tag as creative. Certain individuals will immediately gravitate to this proposal. Their internal patterning, beliefs and values know that a creative solution is precisely what we need in this moment.

Just as quickly, however, others will dismiss this proposal. By tagging it as creative, they will attach a volume of associated meaning to it. In their mind, the word 'creative' is code for hair-brained, impractical, or reckless. They may think to themselves, "Here we go again. I've seen this movie before." Those with low filters simply say it out loud. Either way, they are strongly influencing the neurology of the entire room. The situational context.

But what they have done is reveal something about their own internal wiring. It is useful to finding the path forward. I'll shift the nomenclature, and instead tag the path as 'clever'. This may be enough to keep us moving forward, because it is a characterization that better aligns with their worldview, which goes something like this: Business is a dog-eat-dog world. There are winners and there are losers. Those who are most clever win the game. They find the angle. They use leverage in their favor. They can outfox others.

This subtle shift in semantics may now enable us all to move up the hill towards the prize. Together. Simply by mapping the semantics to the collective beliefs, attitudes and values of those gathered in the room. This is managing the algorithm to improve outcomes.

34

CAUTION

Using stimuli with *The Craft* merits several important words of caution.

First, using the wrong stimuli to help identify the cross-correlations in the algorithm—and their implication for pursuing the highest probability path to achieving optimal value—can reveal the wrong patterns, biases, preferences, and triggers. An inaccurate or flawed read will lower the probability of being able to decode the underlying behaviors within the variables at play and mapping the path forward.

Second, the use of the techniques described in *The Craft* is only for purposes of gaining a truer and more accurate read that informs how to create productive engagement with others who may become or are already part of the company's ecosystem or affect the dynamics of an inflection point. We are simply working to increase our probability of success by understanding the territory before us. These techniques should not be abused or used for any purpose other than for optimizing the path toward achieving optimal value.

Work with honor.

Third, the easiest emotion to stimulate—and the most frequently abused—is fear. It is the feeling that hyperaggressive negotiators use to win deal terms. It is what is used in politics to divide electoral subsegments. It is how insurance is sold.

It is much more difficult to use these stimuli, techniques, and methods for purposes of

bringing people together,

introducing calm into conflict,

sparking creativity, or

enabling people to contribute to a common cause.

These are the noblest uses of these techniques and are reserved for the most gifted of leaders who will leave an enduring legacy of achievement, contribution, and service—true kings.

35

INTELLECT

Most successful people—including corporate executives—believe their success is attributable to their intellect. Other factors that may have contributed to their success—sex, family history, age, era, education, geography, access to ideas and resources, who they intersected with at key moments of their journey, or perhaps sheer coincidence or luck—are discounted.

The self-reinforcing belief is that they have outthought and outmaneuvered all their challengers to achieve their present station.

It is a false belief. It creates a vulnerability or blind spot.

The belief reinforces the perception; the perception reinforces the belief.

The belief will be proven false most often when the situational context changes—either naturally or by provocation.

Your ability to outthink and outmaneuver in whatever game you are playing—whether it be testifying before a regulator, the high-stakes negotiation, the critical media interview, the grilling by disgruntled employees—will be affected as the situational context shifts. Most often, it will be an adverse effect, depending on the nature, speed, and intensity of the shift—and your training and abilities to understand and manage such shifts.

Actually, depending on what specific dimensions of the situational context are shifting, what stimuli are being used, your own intrinsic patterns and conditioning, your preparation, and how this alchemy all takes place, you can transition from being the smartest person in the room to one of the least.

The stimuli can quickly expose what the executive does not know and how they react in unthinking or unknown ways to

    reveal blind spots;

    expose what lurks below the waterline;

    point to where the traps and triggers lie;

    show us how to activate or dull a response; and

    reveal the deeper codes—drawing out the biases, patterns, and triggers that are wired into our cognitive, physiological, and emotional being.

This is how we navigate the challenges and treachery along the path to optimal value. It has little to do with intellect.

PART 4

REVELATION

36

THE SHROUDS

The shrouds are pulled back.

We begin to see the truth.

Now decode the meaning.

Understand the correlations.

Map the path ahead.

37

LOGICAL CONSTRUCTS

Many corporate initiatives underperform their expectations—or simply fall off the rails—because they rely on false assumptions as to how others think, believe, and are motivated to act.

It happens like this:

> The parties come together. The words they all say to one another match up. They see the same arcs. They envision the same outcomes. They share their excitement with one another about the potential of what could be. The wine at the celebratory dinner is memorable.

It will be glorious.

> Then the teams go to work, turning this dream into reality. They work long days and long nights. A few breakthroughs are achieved. A few roadblocks are encountered. The actual vector starts its winding path.

The promoters on the team work to keep spirits up, reiterating the vision, acknowledging the challenges that must inevitably be overcome with any worthwhile goal. But there are murmurs. Soon the dissidents, critics, backbiters and short sellers feel empowered. Most of the ensuing debate—some of it out in the open, some of it behind closed doors—is quite frankly just noise masking something deeper at play.

The something deeper that is bubbling up often pertains to the appropriate allocation of rewards and risk among the various stakeholders touched by the initiative—and their respective responsibilities for getting it done.

The Craft elevates the probability of getting these allocations right by integrating the business strategy and day-to-day tactical execution plan—that is, the aggregation of the business plan, operational model, financial projections, marketing and communications plan, legal structure, and associated fundamentals—with the deeper codes that will truly determine success or failure. There is a direct correlation between that which we are seeking to express above the waterline and that which is at work below. The level and quality of this integration process between the two profoundly affects the path forward—and our probability of success.

Time and time again, executives believe they have alignment among the stakeholders—and have effectively integrated the allocations of risk, reward, and responsibility into the contracts, work orders, project plans, launch plans, matrices of roles and responsibilities, and other operational designs.

Then there is friction, confusion, underperformance, and dispute. The relationship begins to fray. The reason is because of something deeper. Very often the fundamental logical constructs each actor relies on in their own interior architecture are actually quite different, unaligned and unresolved with those held by others. Although the words on the legal documents, business plan, launch strategy, settlement agreement, master services agreement, and so forth, are the same, each of the respective parties believes or assumes something different. People have said things and agreed to things in the moment to close a deal, create an ally, or open an opportunity that don't necessarily reflect what they truly believe. The misalignment surfaces in how they act or react when the pressure is high, or when they feel like the walls are closing in, or their emotions are bubbling up into the forefront to cloud or intensify their perceptions and reactions. The early excitement and memorable wine have masked those assumptions that will later prove invalid.

It happens. A lot. I've invested thousands of hours on tense conference calls and in dreadfully sour conference rooms decrypting the situation to identify the gap. It goes on to cost thousands, millions, and even billions of dollars in lost performance, cost overruns, additional legal and advisory fees, and lost financial potential that could otherwise be harvested in the future. When you scrape away all the noise, confusion, and emotion, it usually traces back to this root— what each fundamentally believes and values is misaligned or even unaligned altogether.

Ironically, very often the parties will do the same thing again the next time they establish a relationship critical to their go-forward strategy, returning to the comfortable grooves of what they know and what the common wisdom tells them. They will have about the same probability of success going forward. Usually though, it is less.

To break this cycle—purposefully and consciously—let everyone know early and often that you are testing the fundamental assumptions about the logical constructs that will underpin the relationship, the contract, the performance expectation, or the next task. This helps ensure three things.

First, when we are looking for the deeper logical constructs and can positively identify them—either in their aligned or unaligned state—it gives us anticipatory advantage—that half-step advantage for understanding what comes next in the game. We are a better player, working at a higher level, because our read is cleaner, quicker, and better informed.

Second, when we are able to identify the competing logical constructs—and the underlying assumptions each of the stakeholders automatically attach to them (a body that may be as broad and deep as a full set of *Encyclopedia Britannica*)—we are able to head off the dissonance that shows up sometime after the memorable wine is finished but before the murmurs, dissidents, and short sellers spin up into a full gale.

Third, when we find ways to align, harmonize, or hybridize the competing logical constructs brought to the table by the various stakeholders touched by the corporate imperative— or build out new ones to rest the corporate imperative on— we move the ball forward efficiently.

The Correlation of Alignment to Financial Performance

This alignment process is the key to successfully building ecosystems around the company—and sparking breakthrough thinking, corporate innovation, creativity, transformation, and reorganization. The alignment process averts a true, often-recurring performance risk.

If you can't expose the underlying logical constructs that the diverse stakeholders bring to the table, your company's attempt to build, innovate, break through, or reorganize will

underperform at best;

deplete the organization of time, energy, and money fighting against the undercurrent; or

simply fail.

In contrast, when you are able to transparently expose these competing logical constructs—and discover a way to adapt or evolve them until they resonate with one another—you are on the path to unleashing the new exponential financial value that can be created by knitting together diverse stakeholder groups within a common ecosystem.

The Influence of Situational Context

The trap of unaligned or mismatched logical constructs can be masked or even fueled by underlying dynamics present within the situational context. For example, every big conference will feature a panel discussion on innovation, disruption, disintermediation, or transformation—it doesn't matter if you are in health care, retail, broadcasting, telecom, or financial services. It will be where all the cool people hang out, fawning on the luminaries, standing in line to ask penetrating questions. Big ideas, bold players.

Much of it is talk. Just words. But people hang on to the ideas and energy and get ensnared. It leads to the intersection between such diverse stakeholders as, for example, those at the conferences wearing hoodies and those in pinstripes. Within this situational context, they will often believe they have found alignment and can knit a path forward together. Unfortunately, their alignment is likely only at a surface level. The initial burst of energy and excitement is masking misalignment. The problems will manifest later—after the deals are done.

Here's why. Stereotypically, the pinstripe crowd is focused on sustaining cash-creating machines while the hoodie crowd works on all the cool stuff. The stuff that is cutting edge. The magic new technology. Where the unicorns are born.

Those two worlds romanticize each other, with the pinstripe crowd hoping to use the hoodies to pour some nitrous into the fuel tank of their machine. The hoodie crowd dreams of the phenomenal exit where they become extraordinarily wealthy because of what they were able to do for the pinstripe crowd.

I've worked with companies ranging from large multinationals to Silicon Valley start-ups, often at the intersection of where these two diverse groups dream of a path forward together. They think differently. There is a lot of sniffing and cuddling—but they don't often breed well. Their deeper codes are different. The underlying beliefs, values, attitudes, and motivations are not aligned.

To illustrate, with two of the corporate spinouts I've led, there were small nodes of extraordinary innovation occurring deep within large companies. In both instances, those large companies knew several things:

First, these nodes were doing some really cool stuff, and as industry experts, they knew they could have a radical transformative effect on the markets they were in.

Second, they were a drain on the parent companies' P&L month over month, depressing margins, limiting the company's own growth and investment options.

Third, these pockets of innovation were taking up too much of the CEO's time at the quarterly board meeting, explaining what the group really did and whether it was valuable or a drag on profit margins.

The best path forward in both cases was to birth these nodes as new companies begun by the pinstripes crowd but then led by the hoodie crowd. They were hard births. There was a fair bit of blood and there was screaming, but something new was created. Everyone fawned over the potential of what it could become.

Then the murmurs started, followed by the fighting. The underlying logical constructs of the pinstripe crowd and the hoodie crowd were misaligned. The words on the legal documents were the same. Everyone read them. Everyone agreed to them. But what they were thinking was very different.

To the hoodie crowd, what was birthed was an infant, full of promise but noisy, messy, and vulnerable. It would require care and feeding and tons of love and affection. This would take years, but it would be worth it. This infant would grow up to be a phenomenal citizen who a mother and father could be extraordinarily proud of one day.

To the pinstripe crowd, what was birthed was instead a teenager. It was a bit risky, prone to pushing boundaries and experimenting with God knows what. But they were still fun, and in another year or two they'd be fully formed adults out conquering the world (and making a ton of money.) Hopefully they'd send a few very nice checks home for dear old mom and dad, just as a thank-you for investing early into what will surely become a brilliant success.

What happened in the end, though, was that everyone was disappointed.

For the hoodie crowd, the next step in the pattern after the spinout was to nurture, feed, and burp the newborn. They would set up a 529 account and harvest the yield years from now. This is what parents should do for their children, the thinking goes.

In contrast, for the pinstripe crowd, it was time to work on budgeting with this reckless teenager, teaching them a lesson that a penny saved was a penny earned. "They'll thank us later."

Both sets of assumptions proved incorrect. It led to underperformance. The innovators never could access enough capital to go the distance properly. The parent corporations could never harvest a meaningful return from the investments they made in gestating the innovation.

Optimal value was never attained.

When two contrasting logical constructs are juxtaposed against each other, everyone ends up disappointed.

More Lessons

There are four additional lessons from this illustration.

First, the stimuli used early to provoke this exploration will lead to an initial and fundamental determination of whether there should be a force of resonance or a force of repelling—both being financially valuable to the companies involved.

Second, what should have happened is a coming together of the counterparties to decode the respective logical constructs early and to find the path to aligning these constructs—even if it means conceding that their own are inadequate. What should happen is a new, higher-evolved, aligned version of constructs that is mutually created and mutually agreed. By reaching in and pulling up this foundational code among the stakeholders setting forth on a journey together—who will walk into any number of forthcoming inflection points together arm and arm—this practice leads to

pathways that are more creative,

ideas that are more advanced,

shared logical constructs positioned to achieve a higher state,

true innovation, and

the creation of exponential financial value.

It is imperative to peel away the words, dynamics, and self-righteousness of the parties until you find underlying structures of unaligned or misaligned logical constructs. Doing so reveals where deeper and often intractable sentiments lie and where work must be done to achieve agreement, cohesion, shared gain, shared risk, cooperation, transformation, and change. Too often the push to make a sale, close a negotiation, craft a transition plan, or establish a relationship is in such haste, under such pressure, or, quite frankly, intentionally pursued with blinders on that the deeper roots of real performance risks that lurk below are never revealed.

Third, the use of the stimuli early also reveals exceptional insight into the likely behavior of the actors when the inevitable dynamics of noise, confusion, and pressure emerge down the road as inflection points are encountered. The stimuli will reveal how various parties engage, battle, accelerate, disengage, become passive-aggressive, sabotage, or exhibit other patterns, biases, or behaviors—including what conditions provoke them to not think but instead to simply react.

Finally, when there is underperformance or failed performance against the original objective (optimal value), the parties will typically walk away from the experience fully satisfied that they were the ones who were right and the others were wrong. It certainly happened with the hoodie crowd and the pinstripe crowd.

This is often the case when people fight but can't see the

misaligned logical constructs at play below the surface. The conflict is not a product of the salty words that are exchanged during the conference calls that preceded the conflagration but instead the competing logical constructs.

Each party is certain their worldview is correct and the other is wrong.

It is simpler that way. It reconciles more easily with our own beliefs and perceptions, reducing internal friction and thereby completing the self-reinforcing circle that goes on between beliefs and perceptions.

The fact is that the new organism birthed by the corporate spinout was neither an infant nor a teenager, but the various sides couldn't move off their individually held logical constructs. They created an either/or decision point in their minds and then locked in—with a feeling of righteousness.

This is the easy way. It doesn't make it right.

It doesn't lead to better outcomes. It does not create financial value. In fact, it usually erodes it.

38

ALLOCATIONS

The effective, transparent, and equitable allocation of risks, rewards, and responsibilities among a company's stakeholders—including the myriad of actors in their extended commercial ecosystem—is one of the most critical kernels to unlocking exponential financial value.

Those companies and executives who are unable to conceive, negotiate, and manage these allocations—again, effectively, transparently, and equitably—will be unable to inflect their corporate trajectory higher. This weakness will manifest when the company encounters the critical inflection points along its vector in pursuit of achieving optimal value. When the allocations are poorly conceived, misaligned, or inflexible, they create drag on the company, its stakeholders, and the initiative by adding pressure, conflict, and drama to the situational context.

Because these allocations are imperative to increasing the probability of success, they must be conceived and designed well—from the very outset—and continuously managed along the vector.

The deeper codes within these allocations are integral to the functioning of the relationships between the company and its stakeholders, as they inform the implicit exchange necessary among individuals, groups, or companies. The codes must be integrated into:

> well-designed commercial contracts and corporate transactions, including investments, acquisitions, sales, mergers, financings, product and service offerings, service agreements, warranties, SLAs, and so forth; and

> the broader exchanges that take place between a company and its stakeholders—both overtly and subtly—including, for example, corporate announcements, policy initiatives, dispute resolutions, and any other proposal, offer, position, or representation made into the market by the company or its executives.

This is simply because these codes tickle at something deeper within the stakeholders. They activate against the beliefs, values, motivations, patterns, and perceptions of the individual. It stirs within them, creating responses and reactions that are cognitive, emotional, or even physiological. They may activate immediately and express as a posture or reaction overtly, or they may simply lie in wait. But if stirred well and assessed accurately, they will reveal how the stakeholders or other actors across the table perceive, react to, and think about the relationship, their behavior, or their performance going forward.

When the codes are aligned with the explicit or implicit allocation of risks, rewards, and responsibilities in the exchange made by the company, they provide the foundation for a healthy ecosystem that can then realize the full financial value it creates. If not aligned, any of these resultant effects will have a deleterious influence on the company's immediate P&L—and hinder the company's potential for creating exponential financial value in the future.

Tactically speaking, these deeper codes tell me a lot— quickly, subtly, and unobtrusively.

> They will tell me whether, for example, in the context of an explicit commercial opportunity, this deal or sale will get done, if at all.

> If something is possible, then they tell me the structure and terms of the offer, proposal, plan, or position going forward that will be necessary to get mutual agreement.

> Finally, once revealed, the codes will tell me whether an issue is going to take an hour to resolve—or a day, a month, or never.

There is something else that can be even more profound once revealed. The deeper beliefs, values, attitudes, and motivations that inform how the allocations could or should be made tell me if the folks sitting on the other side of the conference room table or on the other end of the conference call are the ones I am going to be betting on—or betting against.

Reward Coding

The first code exposes how those actors or stakeholders think about the allocation of rewards in this exchange. Their preference will be wired in very deeply—down into the fabric of their fundamental beliefs and values.

There are three potential options. Do they take the rewards for

themselves (I),

their tribe (we), or

their cause (idea)?

Illustration 12

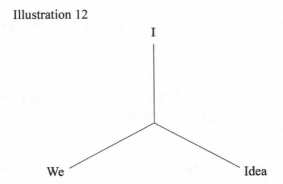

You can identify their primary orientation by asking yourself in your quiet contemplation of the prospective exchange the following question:

Who are they fighting for?

This question is almost primal in its phrasing. Don't listen to the words they are saying. Many have developed the gift to wax eloquently about collaboration, collective success, rising waters lifting all boats, or their commitment to innovation, transformation, progress, and the like—the words used with the *we* or *idea* orientation. Often these words mask what really lies below the waterline.

Many are wired to take for themselves first. They demonstrate a primary motivation toward the *I*. Others seek to first serve their group, indicating a primary motivation toward the *we*. A minority are committed to a cause, passion, or idea, a primary motivation toward the *idea*. Cut through the mask by simply asking, "Who are they fighting for?"

It says something odd on the back cover of this book. It says, "This Is How We Make Kings." Kings lead in vision—but also by demonstrating service and sacrifice. They serve the tribe. Too often senior executives with a predominating orientation to serve their *I* instead of the *we*—the tribe that is their company—are ineffective and short lived. For example, the deals they make with their employees are unsatisfactory to the employees, disincentivizing performances or even creating frustration or revolt. The belief of the *I*-based CEO is unable to build the coalitions, support, and motivation necessary to enable the *we* portion of the tribe to power the ship forward. CEOs who are true kings find the way to serve all—the *I*, the *we*, and the *idea*.

Illustration 13

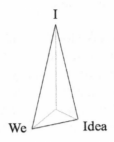

Next, after identifying the primary—even primal—orientation of the person or the group, figuratively speaking—on the other side of the table to your prospective exchange, a degree of granularity can then be added into your read.

The three variables at play within this reward code can be positioned as a triangle with a rubber band around the three points. They then morph with the individual or group so that one and only one variable predominates, and the other two variables manifest as secondary or tertiary in their importance. As one variable increases in importance or predominance, the relative value of one or both other variables must decrease. For example, an individual may be in primary service to their *I* need but then feel a secondary obligation to serve their tribe—*we*—or even to a cause or *idea* (a motivation that can be strongest among some entrepreneurs, innovators, and socially motivated individuals pursuing health, environmental, or welfare-related objectives).

Illustration 14

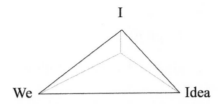

Gathering this secondary assessment will result in an even tighter refinement of your read and be of direct relevance to how you structure your exchange, whether it be

the structure of your sales proposal,

the way you design and describe your new employee incentive program, or

the policy agenda you advance.

The objective for the CEO and senior executive team is to find a relative balance between the three variables—that blend of rewards allocated across the three primary focal points—with enough allocated to the *I* to incentivize inspired leadership at the top, enough allocated to motivate the body of the tribe—the *we*—and enough allocated to the *idea* necessary to fuel the passion needed to pursue not merely margin production but instead unlocking exponential financial value.

Risk and Responsibility Coding

The second deeper allocation code pertains to the way the

actor perceives, reacts to, and thinks about risk as well as the corresponding responsibility associated with the assumption of this risk.

This is a two-step inquiry.

First, we are seeking to decode the following questions:

> Do they push into risk, sensing an opportunity, embracing it, getting jazzed by the challenge of navigating through it?
>
> Or do they seek to minimize their risk—or simply steer clear of it—at every opportunity?

The answer to these questions will fundamentally determine how you approach, create, negotiate, propose, and reconcile with those on the other side of the table.

To get down into the core of this code, ask yourself this primal question:

> *When there is a conflict in the future, whose problem do they think this will be?*

In their mind, what is their answer?

Then, to add depth to your first read, answer the following questions:

> If this is their responsibility, do they step up?
>
> How do they step up?

Will they be successful?

This determines how—if at all—they will map into your ecosystem.

There is a second step. It will reveal even more—digging deeper into the underlying beliefs, values, attitudes, and motivations—and improving the quality and texture of your read.

It pertains to the allocation of risk assumed relative to the rewards taken. It is a proportionality test. Ask yourself:

Are they seeking to harvest a reward that is disproportionate to the risk they assume?

Evaluating how others conceptualize the proportionality between the allocation of rewards to risk in the exchange is not just a negotiating point. This second step will often reveal both if these are parties you want in your ecosystem and whether they will remain aligned with the objective of the exchange throughout the term of the relationship, including when it gets tough.

Which it will.

39

HORIZON

At the beginning of the process of developing the sketch, we determined the initial parameters of time. We established—at least our best prognostication of—the length of time that it will take to achieve the optimal value.

Time has even deeper layers we want to expose. We want to draw these deeper layers out for the simple reason that they are integral to understanding the interior architecture of how different individuals perceive, react, and think within differing or alternative situational contexts. By exposing these layers, we gain a much more meaningful read on the path forward and on our probability of success in extracting exponential financial value. For example, drawing out these layers will reveal how the actors

believe benchmarks should be set and measured for progress along the actual vector;

interact with or react to the alternative events within various inflection points—which manifest differing tensions, paths to resolution, and opportunities to find gold in the midst of change and confusion; and

will be emotionally activated in response to time-based triggers—manifesting alternatively as, for example, excitement, impatience, frustration, anger, malaise, or otherwise.

By revealing these deeper layers, the nature and quality of a prospective relationship within your commercial ecosystem is exposed. The more fundamental codes can then be associated with underlying beliefs, values, attitudes, and biases—and they can be correlated to the allocation of risk, reward, and responsibilities set forth in the business terms and working model.

To reveal these deeper layers, simply ask yourself:

How long is their horizon?

Some individuals or groups need to see an outcome in the next day, week, or month. This short-term lens is sometimes due to the objective needs of the business—an exterior motivation. They need the cash. They need a quick win. But it may also indicate an interior architecture favoring short-term perspectives. As a result, these executives tend to be more transaction oriented in their exchanges with others—which may be entirely appropriate depending on their function within the ecosystem, so long as it is also commensurate with the rewards, risks, and responsibilities they will be allocated. This short-term orientation will define how frequently there will be a need to measure progress and receive rewards, how long they will be patient when KPIs or benchmarks are delayed, and at what point their trust in a relationship will quite simply melt down. For purposes of *The Craft*, what we are doing by stimulating a psychographic variable like horizon is simply mapping the inflection points which will soon and inevitably be encountered on the vector forward.

At the other end of the temporal spectrum are long-termers. At their most extreme point, they envision glorious achievements that will be realized years from now. Many entrepreneurs and bleeding-edge innovators have this DNA strongly within their interior beliefs, attitudes and worldviews.

Between these two extremes are many shades of gray. Each gradation within this realm of grayness will correlate to a different set of allocations—expressed in timelines for expectations, timelines for actual performance, alternative risk assumptions, the appropriate governance model, how friction is managed, the frequency of communications, and the capabilities and personalities of the members assigned.

I have been involved in three corporate spin-offs. In each case, the parent was engaged in businesses which generated strong cash flows ranging from $40 million to $3 billion per annum. While their annual revenues were significant, each one managed their businesses on a quarterly, monthly and even bi-weekly basis. In other words, each stewarded their business with quite short-term outlooks. When they spun off a new company, it was to achieve a bold, potentially disruptive objective that could generate significant financial value. This was exciting, and promised them a potential spot on the marquee with other great entrepreneurial founders. However, pursing a high-value, disruptive path forward necessitates possessing a long temporal horizon. It will take years. Any capital generated will be reinvested into the business. It will not be harvested for short-term gain. In each of these cases, the fundamental belief wired deeply into the senior executives was challenged to bridge a short-term, harvest-oriented wiring in favor of a long-term, reinvestment-oriented wiring. In fact, their short temporal lens was a material drag on the business. In the end, it precluded their ability to achieve their lofty financial aspirations.

40

EMOTIONAL RESONANCE

A lot of learning is from the rearview mirror—the kind no book or lecture can teach. You have to experience it to understand it. Only then can you see the patterns, understand the insights, and begin putting words to it all.

Those who fear entering into new or challenging experiences—such as launching into a new vector or encountering a challenging inflection point—never pass through the portal. They are held back by their fears, including their fear of

the unknown,

losing something never gained,

how others will perceive them, or

the risk of being wrong.

In the corporate context, fears like these hold back the

organization—from new thinking, new workflows, new business models, and new relationships. It is difficult to create exponential financial value when there is fear of entering into those new or challenging experiences that have the potential to create immensely valuable insights—the kind that can be fully understood only once they are in the rearview mirror.

My search into the rearview mirror has been really to learn what it was that determined when we were winning versus when we were losing.

The answer is that we win more often when we anticipate the tripwires that will be encountered—and we anticipate them before all others. Many of the tripwires I discovered while working on the legal, regulatory, financial, technological, and reputational issues for some of the largest corporations, banks, and brands in the world were just that—legal, regulatory, financial, technological, or reputational. This seems obvious.

Just as frequently, the tripwires were something less obvious. They were wired into human nature. The tripwires were tied into the psychological, emotional, or even neurological reactions of the actors. Yet no one wanted to talk about it in a meaningful way or to figure out how to manage it.

The second lesson learned, therefore, was that it was imperative to find these tripwires, draw them out, decode them, and integrate a method for how to deal with them in a more informed, more sophisticated way with our paramount business strategies.

There is a third lesson. The line between winning and losing is often drawn by whether a new proposition, idea, offer, concept, or approach triggers a desired emotional response in the recipient. In your own quiet contemplation of what is going on within an inflection point, ask the following question:

What do they feel?

Feelings are a powerful catalyzing agent. When we find the feeling that can underpin emotional resonance, we find that

> things dormant now come alive,

> things that were just quietly idling at 50 rpm now start cycling at 2,000 rpm, or

> things that we didn't know mattered to us now do.

Sometimes this is a good thing. Sometimes it isn't.

Feelings can break the hold on whatever is stopping people from breakthrough thinking, risk-taking, or assuming higher-performance modes of behavior.

Getting a clean read on the correlated reactions, behaviors, and patterns to emotional resonance—activating them, for better or for worse—is critical to determining when we are on a path of winning versus losing.

Many CEOs and senior executives are not masters of the feelings game. In fact, they'd like to seal them off or keep them safely out of sight below the waterline.

The thinking often goes that it is easier to see clearly and to make tough decisions—the kind of decisions that you know are going to cause someone some pain, somehow, some way—if we seal off those feelings. Fair enough.

However, pushing this awareness below the waterline to seal it off creates a weakness—not a strength.

When managed in an unsophisticated way—or when they simply never become part of the calculation—feelings can hit emotional tripwires that can result in backlash, resistance, or withdrawal.

They can also act as a powerful catalyst in the pursuit of optimal value—when done well.

41

TRUST

Trust is a deep code. In the context of business, it is much discussed. It is poorly understood. Trust is one of the most challenging codes for companies and executives to decipher, and then honor and respect. As previously noted, it is one of the tripwires that ends in a conflagration for many.

Within the context of *The Craft*, our objective is to release exponential financial value for the company by aligning and integrating the deeper codes drawn from the beliefs, values, attitudes, motivations, and biases of the individual actors with the larger corporate strategy. As we have established, this objective is pursued along two primary paths:

First, this methodology is essential to knitting together the broader commercial ecosystems around the company necessary for creating and realizing new sources of financial value, including those sources of value sparked by such transformative changes in the marketplace as technological innovations, opportunities for improved resource allocation, and the development of innovative business models that leverage existing assets and capabilities in new ways.

Second, this methodology enables us to successfully manage through the critical inflection points—and the myriad of dynamics that affect the behaviors within these inflection points—that will be encountered on the company's journey from where they are today to that point of optimal value in the future.

In either case, trust is a deeper code that will determine your path, the quality of the journey, and your probability of success in reaching the door to the other side.

Trust is a quality knit into the fabric of a fundamental belief integral to how we create our commercial exchanges and the relationships that determine their success or failure:

You can take me someplace I otherwise cannot go.

To understand trust as an integral element of this deeper belief, there are two underlying variables that must be decoded. Both variables must be activated prior to the relationship bonding together and then remain positively activated throughout its term. If either one of the variables is invalidated at any point, trust will dissipate or disappear. This is when the relationship will suffer, tensions will rise, drag ensues, and the probability of successfully achieving the optimal value is reduced.

The "Like Us" Variable

The first variable is similarity—the actors or parties must establish that the other is "like us."

Like us does not mean those who are of a similar sex, race, ethnicity, sexuality, nationality, religion, or any other distinctions humans use to define, delineate, or divide themselves, including to gain advantage over or otherwise denigrate others.

Like us, in the context of *The Craft*, means those with whom you share common beliefs, values, attitudes, and motivations as they pertain to the prospective exchange or allocation of rewards, risks, and responsibilities. To trust another in the give-and-take exchanges of these relationships, there must be a level of commonality, familiarity, and comfort that the way one perceives, reacts, and thinks is similar to the other—it enables the familiar rhythms and measure of predictability in what we expect others to do.

The Consistency Variable

The second variable is consistency. Once a party is assured that the other perceives, reacts, and thinks in a manner similar enough to their own to meet the qualification of being like us—call it perceptual resonance—then these familiar patterns, rhythms, and expectations must be consistently experienced. To state this in the inverse, when we think we know someone, but then their manifestations indicate something different—either through words or action—we lose trust in our assumption. It can become the slippery slope leading to lost trust in the other party.

For example, imagine a large corporation spending the better part of the last year evaluating different options for a new technology platform. They talked with all the relevant vendors, saw the demos, heard the pitches, and negotiated with several before selecting one. The winning vendor had great technology. It is now a major component of the company's five-year strategy to emerge in its market among the top three competitors. Internal analyses indicate that this new technology platform should enable the company to realize a 20 percent compound annual growth rate while becoming substantially more efficient—the technology will enable the company to harvest data from its extended supply chain, providing insights that will be used by the manufacturing department to better calibrate production and inventory levels, by the marketing department to improve the ways in which the company speaks to its customers, and by operations to root out inefficient workflows and poor-performing business units. As part of the extensive due diligence and negotiations between the company and the vendor, the senior executives came to know one another extremely well. They each had worked at it, as both were committed to the notion that to create a long-term relationship like the one envisioned, they must come to understand each other's perspectives. The deal was signed. Several bottles of memorable wine were shared. There were toasts to the glorious days ahead.

It is now six months later. There are problems with the implementation. The collaborative teams between the vendor's and the company's personnel are no longer collaborative. In fact, many have devolved into outright dysfunction. Key dates are being missed. There is significant miscommunication. The charismatic salesperson who shepherded the sale has been flitting in to check on things and then disappearing when the conversations grow heated. Other executives are dancing around, all trying to appear responsive without becoming responsible.

The deeper challenge in this moment is one of consistency. The company had grown to trust the vendor—gaining confidence that they knew how the vendor perceived things, how they would react to various conditions, and how they think.

The vendor had done the same. They made a big bet on this horse in the race—agreeing to not take on certain projects with this company's primary competitors, cutting their margins, and taking a significant portion of their payment based on future performance.

The mutual assumptions made by both parties are eroding. So, too, is their level of trust.

Events like this happen. Always.

They should be anticipated. Always.

There should be a game plan already in place for this eventuality. Always.

There rarely is.

The conditions will likely devolve further.

The actual path of this vector is attributable in significant part to the ways in which trust was originally established. Each of the parties came to rely on the assumption that the other was like us. However, when subjected to the pressure, noise, confusion, and dynamics of the inflection point—a predictable event—the assumption was no longer consistently expressed. The words now sound different. The actions look different. We perceive they are no longer like us. They are hedging. Dodging. Ghosting. Dancing. Lying. We conclude, "We don't trust them."

The cross-perceptions of the other party will soon devolve to another conclusion. It rests in the comfort of righteousness. It is a belief activated well below the waterline. It is not spoken, yet it profoundly affects the interior lens through which the actors now navigate the inflection point. "They are less than us." It is common—particularly within those inflection points resulting in the flat, stalled, or descending arcs of companies that have failed to manage their way through. It is a righteous sentiment that exclusively serves the ego of the beholder. It rarely is useful to building high-value—or to creating functionally viable—commercial relationships.

The primary belief underlying trust—at least in commercial contexts like this—is that the other party can take us places we cannot otherwise go. When the underpinnings of this belief are questioned or invalidated—because the perception is that the beliefs, values, attitudes, and behaviors originally relied on have shifted or are shifting—trust dissipates quickly. It may even disappear.

42

REVOCABLE LICENSE

To create exponential financial value within companies—ranging from global multinationals all the way through to entrepreneurial innovators—it takes a network of many differentiated skills and capabilities knit together brilliantly in order to unlock the significant value promised.

This is imminently challenging alchemy.

With trust, we looked for the variable of others being like us. Now we look for differentiation.

Differentiation is the second ingredient to support the fundamental belief we need in our commercial exchanges:

> *You can take me someplace*
> *I otherwise cannot go.*

Differentiation is necessary to the relationship because we rely on you to provide your differentiated value—what we do not possess ourselves to achieve optimal value.

This differentiated value may be obvious—for example, providing a capital asset, distribution channel, or financing.

More often, particularly when the objective is not just to generate a margin but instead to unlock exponential financial value—the differentiated value we desire is something different—it is more ethereal. We need their vision. We need their unique perception. They think in a different way. They put all the pieces of the puzzle together in a different way—which is corporate innovation. It is breakthrough thinking. It is transformation. It does lead to disintermediation, disruption, and corporate trajectories that climb higher. It does unlock exponential financial value.

We desire the comfortable rhythms and predictability of those like us, but simultaneously we need them to be different from us. It is necessary to the health and vitality of our ecosystem. It puts us on a path to achieve optimal value.

At the level of deeper coding that goes on in creating high-value commercial relationships, at least metaphorically speaking, we give them a license to be different from us.

This license, however, is revocable. We attach strings to it. We allow others to be different from us in the commercial context so long as this differentiation is valuable to our journey. When the differentiation is simply different from us but provides little to no value to our ability to manage through inflection points or to otherwise achieve optimal value, we reserve the right to revoke the license.

The revocable license operates below the waterline. It is not consciously expressed. It is not in the legal agreements. But it is there, ever present—profoundly affecting how the parties communicate, perceive, react, and think. To manage its influence on the path of the actual vector, draw this deeper code up above the waterline for yourself and your team. Draw it out with others who may be or become part of your journey. By exposing this deeper code to the sunlight— revealing it transparently as a dynamic in the cognitive and emotional experience of the journey together—we create stronger relationships at the outset. This increases the probability of our success along the vector toward optimal value.

PART 5

CASE STUDIES

43

BEHIND CLOSED DOORS

CEOs and senior executives work largely within controlled conditions. Their speeches are prepared. Their events are scripted. Their schedules are highly organized. Their operational meetings are predictably recurring. Their most significant decisions are made behind closed doors. By controlling the conditions around the decisions, corporate risk is minimized—legally, reputationally, and financially.

Illustration 15

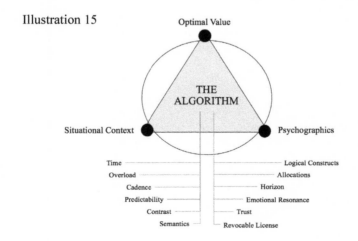

Unfortunately, these controlled conditions shield most from understanding what it is that separates those companies that are able to create exponential financial value from those that cannot—those that are winning from those that are losing. Without access to what it is that happens behind those closed doors, how decisions are made, what influences them, and how the underlying psychographic dimensions of the actors percolate up to determine ultimate outcomes, most walk blind, committing the same errors made by others over and over. A more widely accessible understanding of the cross-correlations between some of the most determinative variables affecting major corporate decisions and long-term financial outcomes proves elusive.

To better understand how the methodology and techniques of *The Craft* yield an understanding of those deeper codes most determinative of outcomes, two case studies are provided—one involving a public company and the other a private company.

44

PUBLIC COMPANY CASE STUDY

We rarely get to see senior executives battle in the arena before the crowds—where it is raw and the truth is revealed. One of the rare instances when we do is the congressional hearing. It is the arena where I began my career.

My job was to prepare these executives in the yard outside the arena before releasing them into the public spectacle that awaited. It was an early glimpse into my study of the ways in which corporate executives perceive, react, and think in those moments in which the noise, pressure, and confusion was high—often intentionally so. It is not an arena designed for them to win. Instead, it is designed to entertain the masses.

I worked to carefully craft their narrative, mock out the scenarios, develop the game plan and contingencies, and then run the executives through the paces, trying to break them down within the safe confines of a conference room on K Street—carefully controlled conditions preceding what would come next.

It was close to the nerve—a place where I get to see people at their best—and their worst. Which is what conditions like this do to people: they amplify, distort, and often reveal the truth of who they really are, in this moment, with no artifice, no NDAs, no advisers out front blocking, and no security desk to pass through.

Most executives will never face a congressional hearing. But they will face demanding scrutiny where the sunlight gets very, very bright. They will

be questioned as to their motivations and objectives;

feel the ratchet tighten as their decisions are picked apart by others, with the prospect of being told that they are wrong or that they are lesser; and

feel the butterflies—activating in some the urge to fight while in others, the urge to flee.

Stimuli used in situational contexts like this and that affect us markedly at the neurological, emotional, and even physiological levels reveal the cross-correlations that determine when we are winning and when we are losing.

Context

Facebook faced a challenging year in 2018. The technology behemoth was at the center of the controversy involving US election influence, the spread of fake news, and the misuse of users' data—including by Cambridge Analytica. These specific events also gave rise to broader, more fundamental concerns about social media, how information could be widely disseminated and, specifically, how opinions were shaped, and other critical dimensions of how people today come to perceive, react, and think about political, social, cultural, and other issues.

One of the critical inflection points endured by Facebook in managing through these challenges was CEO Mark Zuckerberg's testimony before committees of the US Senate and the US House of Representatives. The opportunity to grill corporate executives in front of television cameras is prized by politicians. There is a playbook for how to do it. Some politicians become brilliant at the game, using it as their launchpad for an introduction to broader audiences— particularly important for those who aspire to higher office.

At the most fundamental level, the objective for the CEO is to come off as caring, compassionate, responsible, and trustworthy. If achieved, they then hope it helps to defuse tension, lower the level of scrutiny, forestall any legislative or policy-based rebuke, comfort financial markets, and assuage consumers that they are not another self-serving corporation that subscribes to the greed-is-good ethos.

The objective of the politicians is to prove the opposite. They earn points by demonstrating that neither Facebook nor Zuckerberg can be trusted—either a little bit or a lot. Tearing at the notion of trust earns points with an audience at home—and can become their subsequent justification for increasing regulatory oversight and controls.

As a first insight, note that although there are objectives that will play out above the waterline—for example, forestalling legislative or regulatory consequences, precluding a loss of shareholder value, and so forth—the way in which the points are actually scored in the game turns on something deeper—a perception of being caring, compassionate, responsible, and trustworthy. In other words, whether the CEO is winning or losing turns on how well those dimensions that are anchored below the waterline—beliefs, values, attitudes, motivations, biases, and preferences—resonate with the audience. When there is alignment among these deeper codes and the substantive agenda above the waterline—we can feel that resonance—the CEO will succeed, both personally and in service to the company. Warren Buffett, for example, demonstrated this alignment between what is above and below—including through his congressional testimony—in the wake of the Salomon Brothers fiasco in the early 1990s.

Zuckerberg faced the exact same test—because in this moment, regardless of Facebook having a market cap in excess of $450 billion, the outcome of this inflection point turns on our read of a single man—and who he is at a deeper level, without packaging, without the prepared narrative, and without any regard to what either he or Facebook intend for us to believe. We are looking for the raw truth.

Because the focus is on the performance of a single man—the personification of a much larger entity—the politicians are able to earn bonus points in the scoring by those sitting in the long rows of the arena above if they can make him squirm, stumble, or fall into a trap. In today's media cycles, it is preferable if this foible can be captured in a video clip of fewer than thirteen seconds in length—a nice length for viral memes that will ironically flood constituents' own Facebook newsfeed for the next twenty-four to forty-eight hours.

Stimuli

The situational context is purposefully constructed to increase the intensity of the moment on Zuckerberg. It is designed—after decades of experience—to expose the CEO's performance in ways he cannot consciously control in the moment. It is known that when CEOs cannot control the moment—a vulnerability of those who live in brilliantly managed, carefully controlled environments—we may see the truth. It is a way to access what it is below the waterline. We stimulate the patterns to reveal everything that comes next, including the following questions:

How do they perceive what is going on all around them?

How do they manage what they can control and what they can't?

How well do they manage the fire?

Do they fight?

Do they run?

Do they quit?

In these situational contexts, there are wizards at work behind the screen identifying the patterns so that they can better understand how the situational context and stimuli can be further adjusted to provoke the next reaction. Whether it is the staffer sitting in the row behind that senator, a prosecutor going after a corporate executive for fraud, or a clever negotiator putting together a big deal, they practice a shared craft. They are asking,

What is the pattern?

What is the reaction we desire?

How do we provoke it?

They are seeking to reveal what lies below the waterline.

Revelations

Practicing *The Craft* reveals several interesting dimensions key to understanding Zuckerberg and Facebook emanating from the situational contexts and psychographic dimensions of the experience. These will certainly influence what comes next for the company. They may, in fact, determine it.

The first revelation pertains to allocations. With regard to the variable of reward coding, there is misalignment. We are seeking to understand the actor's primary motivation: Who are they fighting for? In the context of Facebook—like a lot of Silicon Valley companies—they use the words of the *we*, or a communal orientation, or, alternatively, the *idea*, or a passion orientation. It is viewed as more noble and perhaps more consistent with the ethos of the significant number of highly educated millennials within this ecosystem. In the context of Facebook, however, the largest shareholder is Zuckerberg. He is the CEO, founder, and chairman of the board. He controls the voting rights of the company. There is a tremendous amount of *I* in the governance of Facebook, and it roots down into the beliefs, values, and attitudes of Zuckerberg, the man. He and Facebook are indivisibly one. Efforts by institutional shareholders subsequent to the congressional hearings to reduce his influence over the company—to create more separation between the man and the company—have been blocked. This is an *I* company, not a *we* company. This revelation ties closely to the second one—trust.

Trust is tested on two operative variables in commercial contexts like this: Are you like us, and is this consistently expressed? Collectively, if both questions are answered in the affirmative, it supports the belief that you can take us someplace we otherwise cannot go—a commercial exchange may proceed and endure. This is a challenge for Zuckerberg. It is personal. He does not engender a feeling that he is like us. He feels alien to us. He moves differently. He struggles to connect. He drinks water differently from us.

We may allow it—for Zuckerberg to be different—because we allow geniuses to be different. We excuse his ill-fitting suit, bangs cut too straight, and uncomfortable presence within his own mortal body. We permit him a license to be different. We embrace his genius but only so long as it takes us someplace we otherwise cannot go. Facebook as a social network tool has certainly enabled this for billions of people—to go someplace and experience something they otherwise could not have done alone. But our license is revocable—we can take it away if we are not provided with commensurate value. This is the deal.

Meaning

Facebook is on a long vector. It is winding. It has created tremendous wealth and value for many shareholders. It is now working through challenging inflection point after challenging inflection point—each one of which has the ability to shift the arc of the company, even flattening or causing it to descend.

The company's probability of success in this challenge—and ensuring the sustained growth of this arc—can be improved by tackling two deficiencies identified by *The Craft*.

First, evolve Facebook so that it better embraces the we orientation as a social platform truly focused on creating networks of communication and community—but in a safe, transparent, privacy-assured fashion. Today Facebook is built on an *I* orientation that is harvesting data and monetizing it, with historically poor safeguards over the purpose or nature of such use. This will be a difficult transition for the company to make, as its shareholders have come to expect a rate of return for this historical business practice. Evolving its model to a higher order will involve conflict with key stakeholders. But the long-term sustainability of Facebook's vector depends on it.

Second, the revocable license held by Facebook is contingent on the value it provides. There are indications that user growth is flattening and usage patterns are declining— indicators of users deriving less value from the platform or that Facebook is perceived to be taking a disproportionate reward from the exchange (harvesting personal data and then monetizing it in a fashion where users perceive the benefits of the exchange are disproportionate between them and Facebook). One of the most significant threats Facebook faces—in the wake of abuses of user data, unseemly data-sharing practices, and enabling third-party users to access and abuse such data without integrity or safeguards—is user backlash. If Facebook users do not receive value, they will revoke the license they extend to Facebook and Zuckerberg to be different. It is one of the fundamental codes we build our commercial exchanges on. If you can no longer take me someplace I otherwise cannot go—or the differentiated value is lessened materially for the users—then Facebook's probability of success will be lower.

By studying the Facebook congressional hearings, we are able to reveal the deeper codes at work. It is just one forum, albeit one where we can witness the algorithm at play in a transparent, public way. These same codes operate in the myriad of exchanges with all company stakeholders—every employee, every investor, and every partner. They are asking in each instance, "Do I trust you?" The deeper codes tell them the answer. Sheryl Sandberg, the COO of Facebook and sister of Zuckerberg, knows it too. She said in Davos in January 2018, "We have to earn back trust." It is fundamental. It is one of the deeper codes and is hanging in the balance.

45

PRIVATE COMPANY CASE STUDY

The actual names and certain key details of this case study, along with the other illustrations in this book, have been changed or anonymized to protect confidences.

I was in my office several blocks from Georgetown University. An international number popped up on my mobile. Country code 962.

The voice was that of an Arabic speaker—but the American accent laid on top was quite close to that of a native speaker— making it feel at once both foreign and familiar.

The caller was the favored son of a family who controlled a large private equity investment fund in the Middle East. I had come to know him as the face of the family when they sought out opportunities in the United States and when they negotiated with the Americans.

"He'd like to talk with you," he said.

I'd never met his father—the patriarch. I had only seen his signature. Six months before he had committed this company to spending hundreds of millions of dollars investing in a massive infrastructure project with my sovereign client. It was his signature on the final documents. He was the wizard working from behind the screen.

The agreements were tough. It had taken me nearly a year to figure out the scheme for the tender and concessions. I wanted to lock down any loopholes. I didn't want anyone playing games. I didn't want anyone hiding in dark corners.

I had to work from inside their heads, acting out every game they would play to exploit my weaknesses, finding my blind spots, testing for points of leverage where they would force decisions in their favor, not mine. I had sent out probes and proxies into their ranks and launched minor skirmishes, decoys, and ploys to test how they perceive, react, and think. I, too, had played the wizard behind the screen, pulling levers and punching buttons, enacting the play before us. I knew who the family was.

Or, at least, I thought I did.

They had holdings around the world, and I had crawled into every nook of their legal structures and financials that I could possibly find, probing their friends and enemies, legal databases, the public internet, and the dark web for any clues that might be scattered about.

The family had a distinct calling card among multinational investors. Most global investors run from risk. The family ran toward it. They leaned into the risks of political, military, and economic calamity. It was in their blood. It had become epigenetic, coded into their very DNA. Generation upon generation of the family had experienced cataclysm and had come out the other side stronger—and wealthier.

Context

My next encounter with the investment fund would be different. There would be no screens, neither he behind his nor me behind mine. It would be face-to-face. On his turf. This would better reveal the elusive, ephemeral, and subtle clues as to who each of us was—the kind of revelations that cannot be gained from phone calls or emails. The words can belie the reality. Instead, these are the clues that must be sensed, leading to the deeper codes we were both in search of.

I boarded a flight the next day from Dulles to Amman. After a shower at the Grand Hyatt, a black Chrysler 300 picked me up at the hotel. The driver spoke a bit of English, enough to confirm that he was the right driver and I was the right passenger. His hands were rough with calluses and his shoes were dusty. He was a driver of necessity today, I presumed. When he wasn't dispatched to pick up a guest, I imagined him working in the garden and maintaining the properties.

We wove through Amman's streets, navigating out to a near suburb. The driver parked the 300 near a wooden gate in a narrow alley. A high stucco wall surrounded the property. When I passed through the gate, an expansive view of Amman opened, revealing its rolling cityscape. The dome of the Blue Mosque dominated the view.

The patriarch was already sitting at a metal patio table beneath an olive tree just inside the gate. He was grandfatherly, gentle and warm.

The driver disappeared back into the alley, returning to his other tasks of the day. The patriarch called for the housekeeper to come out from the kitchen. She was slow to respond. He shouted again, this time louder. It felt too gruff. An older Filipino woman shuffled out.

I settled into the chair underneath the tree. "I've been watching you work for a year now," he said.

He had observed how I led an international tender for the past year, dealing out cards one at a time, ultimately generating more than $300 million in returns, or more than twenty times the original target of generating $10 million to $15 million.

He thought he had come to know the better part of me. Yet he now needed to feel my presence and decode my words. It was a new phase in the dance. He needed to get his read on the man who sat across from him.

As did I.

The older woman brought us both lemonade in cold glasses with ice. Just a quiet Sunday in a shady spot a long way from Georgetown.

"I think you could help us."

"Perhaps," I said, careful to again play just one card at a time.

Over three generations, his family had developed a sprawling business empire that extended from the Middle East to the

United States, Europe, Russia, and North Africa.

They had built it with little more than their cunning.

Jordan is a peaceful pocket surrounded by tremendous wealth and hateful war. The way to make money when you live on land that lacks both oil and water, and the way you prevent the wars all around you from engulfing your own peaceful oasis, is by being brilliant at the game. What they do is act as the go-betweens among nations, factions, and families. They shuttle information, favor, material, and money among those who share common interests, economically and politically. They are particularly valuable to those who would otherwise be considered odd bedfellows—Saudis, Israelis, Jordanians, Russians, Algerians, Palestinians, Egyptians, Americans, British, and the stateless NGOs. They map the internecine network of people and power, decrypting the motivations and tripwires that unite and divide them, tugging on the strings to find where money can be made along the way.

They play the game. They take their cut. This is their craft.

Much of what they do is out in the open. It is the front of the store.

Given their craft, however, there is a fair bit they keep in the back. To see what is in the back of the store, you must be asked to pass through the curtains that divide. Most never are. Most do not know the subtle codes that must be whispered to earn passage. Most are too brash, too oblivious, too naive, or too bold to be invited behind the curtains. Secrets are not shared with those not worthy. They are not shared with those who have not mined for the rarest of currencies: trust.

In reality, their business isn't much different from any other company's business. They all keep secrets. They all have a front of the store and a back.

But it is in the back where I want to go. It is where they keep their power. It is where they hide vulnerability. It is where the deeper codes are found.

For the patriarch, whose legacy was successfully built shuttling between the front and the back of those he served— those odd bedfellows who unite only to serve shared economic and political purposes—they were students of the codes kept. Like all of us who play versions of the game, they were jaded, cynical, suspicious, opportunistic, clever, coy, sophisticated, and naive, all at once. As emissaries who worked in the shadows, it was inevitable. For this group, it was amplified so significantly by the extremes where they worked that it had become woven deeply—epigenetically— into their deeper codes. They could not control them, temper them, or shield them. They simply were.

These are the codes I sought. These are the codes that would reveal their worldviews, their patterning, and their tripwires. This is where their truths would lie.

Like many of those I have worked for—whose confidences are comfortably protected behind nondisclosure agreements and legal privilege—there is a pattern:

They aspire. They fear. They want more. It is human.

They want more money. More power. More influence. More recognition.

They are CEOs, innovators, politicians, and investors.

The tripwires are largely human—cognitive, emotional, and even physiological.

Because they are human, the tripwires follow patterns. They are not each unique. Regardless of whether the CEO is the patriarch of an enterprise that mines those conflicts we casually glance over while scanning the New York Times with our morning scone, or the CEO of a Global 1000 company who works from the glassy confines on the fifty-second floor, there will be common patterns as well as secrets and methods for successfully passing through to the other side. The two are not so different. Regardless of title or stature or reputation or geography, the tripwires we find are always there. Because they are alike, we can map the journey, predict what comes next, and improve our probability of reaching the other side.

For the patriarch, his quest now was to immortalize his legacy. To do so, he needed to do more from the front of the house and less from the back. This was his aspiration. He needed public legitimacy. Many others who begin their climb as outsiders reach this same point—to be recognized as a legitimate force. It is a predictable pattern in the journey. It is a difficult one. Many inflection points stand in their way, any one of which, if poorly managed, can cause them to career into the wall midway, stalling or flaming out.

The first step in the patriarch's vector was to register a $1 billion investment vehicle with the investment authority of a Middle Eastern government. With the seal of the regulator emblazoned on his letterhead—a seal as worthy as a Royal

Warrant granted by the British Crown—he had begun in earnest his march toward legitimacy.

It was only the first step, however. It would be perhaps the easiest. He would need help getting through the inflection points that would be encountered to reach the other side.

My suspicion was that he felt he needed someone with an American passport, fair skin, and a SEAL-like frame to help him to do so.

Stimuli

Before he could commit, he would need to see my deeper codes. They must be revealed—including by dropping me into the situational context of extremes, which naturally evokes revelations, reactions, and patterns. The patriarch wanted to find the back of the room I kept.

More specifically, he would then test and sense to see if I was "like us."

I couldn't be squeamish about the challenge or the risk, but instead I embraced it—just like us.

Like us, I had to be able to peer into the darkness of what lies before the turn and envision what could emerge on the other side.

Like us, I would have to be a tough negotiator, for the Arab ethos is built on respect being earned through power and cunning.

He would also test to see how I was different from us. The

patriarch knew there were codes he did not possess. He would pay for someone who could take him places he could not otherwise go—through the passageway to the other side where public legitimacy lies.

> I had to be different from us in that I could do deals in their high-risk markets—where fair dealing and transparency were not the norm—and raise them to an international standard.

> I had to be different from us in that I could elevate the quality and prestige of the relationships and partners in their ecosystem. This would be his proof—well-known corporate logos and deals of high integrity—for demonstrating his worthiness of public legitimacy.

> I had to be different from us in that I could see things in a different way.

> I had to be different from us in that I could create relationships of trust with others, whose own underlying beliefs, values, attitudes, and motivations were not like the patriarch's but more like mine—I could be their intermediary, knitting together the diverse networks they would need across the world necessarily to create exponential financial value for their fund. If I could do this, I could take them places they otherwise could not go alone.

He had watched me from his own darkened shadows put together one of the most challenging commercial ventures in the midst of a war, political chaos, and geo-economic-political wrangling. Now he was seeing me up close and personal, in his own way, for his own purposes. His questions of "Is he like us?" and "How is he different from us?" are the same questions we all ask when we are building trust—or tearing it apart—without regard to language or geography or culture. It is universal.

These are simply part of the codes we must unlock to gain access to our own darkened passageways.

To reveal more, the patriarch was a master of the stimuli, manipulating the notions of time and place. He would introduce new ideas, concepts, players, and conditions quickly, unpredictably, and without seeming order or structure. Then he would watch and listen. He would sense.

The next morning, the driver pulled the 300 onto the tarmac of Queen Alia International Airport. It was just before dawn. The air was still cool. I climbed the stairs into a small, four-seat private jet. He was already seated inside.

An attendant greeted me with a warm smile. She had deep-brown eyes made more striking by dark eyeliner. She was dressed in a flowing silk blouse with bold colors. Her hair was uncovered, and she wore perfectly tailored slacks fitting of a Paris house. She took my blue sport coat and hung it behind the door. She lacked confidence in her English, preferring to use her eyes to communicate. He interrupted my study. "Are you ready?"

"Absolutely."

The plane took off. Through the small window, I watched a handful of goats forage through the dry scrub of the desert below.

Yesterday's lemonade on a warm Sunday afternoon in Amman was lovely, but it was too far away from where he made his money. He needed to get me closer to the edge. He needed to see me in the places where he mined for the kind of outsized returns that would make the unicorn hunters of Silicon Valley blush. He needed to expose my nerve—make it raw—and reveal the truth of who I was.

The sun streamed into the cabin as we crossed the golden Saharan sands below. I tracked our flight path on the monitor: Egypt, Libya, Chad, Niger, Nigeria, and finally into Ghana's capital, Accra.

The plane pulled to a stop on the tarmac forty meters from a side terminal. The cabin filled with hot, wet air as the door opened. A low-level Ghanaian in uniform led us to a discreet entrance. The room inside was painted mint green. Televisions in the corners streamed Ghanaian news. Worn leather couches lined the room. A portrait of the baby-faced Ghanaian king was hung on the wall.

Our passports were taken. Tea was offered. The patriarch and I sat, uncomfortably bored—anxious for some action.

A tall young man in his late twenties arrived. He was in fashionable jeans and an untucked short-sleeve shirt. His big smile and overeager handshake were jittery.

He, too, was family. Just someone else's.

He would be our intermediary while in Ghana, shuffling us among the powers in this local ecosystem of power, influence, and money, pulling on its cords and levers to gain us access and insights into where money might be made and at what cost.

Our read began immediately. Was his authority real? Did he have access? Could he be trusted? Where were his allegiances? Was he playing us? Could he make the play? Was he a decoy? Are we in the game, and is this the game we want to play?

We spent the day in the back of his Land Rover shuttling across Accra, meeting reputed power brokers, businessmen, and useful agents. Some seemed legitimate. Others not. We ended the day watching the setting sun from a beachfront restaurant. Once the darkness stole the view, we moved to the lobby of a local hotel. We sat and waited for hours, end upon end. The intermediary would take us to the president of Ghana tonight.

Several young women sat alone in the lobby, making indirect eye contact as we stretched our legs. They were looking for a subtle nod or a wink. They were young hookers, perhaps simply trying to pay their own way. They may have also been bait set by the powers that be to gain favor or leverage when the time would later arise—stimuli placed into another's game to test reactions and behaviors. It is part of the game.

The intermediary took call upon call on his mobile phone, trotting in and out of the lobby and among a posse of other young Ghanaian men dressed in knockoff, faux-worn designer jeans from China, imitation Italian loafers worn without socks, and shirts buttoned just a bit too low.

The patriarch was growing more and more gruff with the powerless boys appointed to tend to him while in Accra.

"When will we go?" I asked the intermediary every half hour. We were growing impatient with the late hour, the unusual protocol, and a concern that he lacked the juice to make the play.

The intermediary's phone rang again. It was 10:15 p.m. in Accra.

He simply listened and then hung up.

"Let's go," he said in Ghanaian English wrapped in American tones. He, too, had gone to university in the United States. It was the way families groomed their lieutenants, the next generation entrusted to knit together the odd multinational networks that come together for political, military, and monetary gain.

We hustled to the Land Rover parked in the circular drive in front of the hotel. The intermediary shooed one of his guys out of the driver's seat and took the wheel himself. We would meet the president in his personal residence.

The intermediary navigated the Land Rover in and out of traffic and the occasional pedestrian barely visible in the black Accra night. He pulled down a darkened alley, then killed his headlights while rolling the vehicle slowly forward to a small hut. We looked ahead, peering into floodlights rigged to a generator, allowing those peering out from the dark to see our faces. We tried to show calm. I tipped my blue American passport just above the dash to catch its golden seal in the lights.

The intermediary brought the white Land Rover to a stop. We stepped out and walked toward the floodlights.

Two young men in fatigues stood twenty meters away from us at our ten and two o'clock positions. They held AK-47s across their chests. They seemed bored and uninterested.

Six young athletic men in plain clothes approached us, emerging from the floodlights straight ahead. They were hard to see, but I could feel their energy. They were amped up, excited, unpredictable, dangerous. It felt like hyenas circling.

At five meters out, five of them stopped and hung back. I could see the glint off one of their hands. They, too, were armed. I doubted they were trained—merely dangerous and unpredictable. Boys becoming men. Undeveloped prefrontal cortexes. Primal actors.

The sixth continued toward us. If he had been born in the low country of South Carolina instead of in a shack outside of Accra, he would be an All-American defensive end for an SEC school. Six foot seven inches tall. Two hundred eighty pounds. Eight percent body fat. Lightening in his eyes. No gun. If necessary, he would simply beat us.

He patted us down, checking for holsters under our arms, along our lower backs, and down along our ankles. Satisfied, he turned and grunted.

We followed him to the door in the distance. We could hear a television blaring inside. The defensive end and the hyenas stopped just outside the door.

The president of Ghana greeted us at the darkened door.

Revelations

There are four primary revelations from this case study.

First, the patriarch liked shifting the situational context quickly and significantly. It was a test. He wanted to see my responses. He wanted to see my reactions— physiologically, emotionally, and cognitively. He wanted to see my adaptability to changing circumstances. This reveals underlying patterning, including as to the flexibility to move in and out of situations quickly, shift domains of knowledge easily, and interact with new actors quickly and meaningfully. He would probably never put words to it, but what he was working toward was to see if someone could play in his game. Not everyone could. There was a long string of washouts who simply broke from the extreme conditions they faced or he placed on them.

Which leads to the second. The test was to see if I was "like us." Could I move quickly? Could I manage up and down through power levels? Was I discerning of the potential of various counterparties and influencers in a commercial ecosystem that may need to be built? Could I envision the opportunity?

Third, would he extend a revocable license to be part of the commercial ecosystem of this investment fund—because I provided differentiated value to him and to the fund? Could I take them someplace they could not otherwise go, by doing things they otherwise could not do?

Fourth, could he feel it? He—like all of us—needed to find that feeling that this was right. He was testing for emotional resonance—those feelings that tickle at underlying beliefs, values, and attitudes—to activate them.

Meaning

The patriarch found his answers. There was no pronouncement. I simply went on to work in over thirty countries for the investment fund, toggling against the multitude of beliefs, values, attitudes, and motivations of a myriad of actors, doing so early, getting the read, decoding the commercial ecosystem that could be built, making the recommendation, and negotiating the deals that would lead to creating exponential financial value.

PART 6

APPLICATION IN THE REAL WORLD

46

THE END GAME

Those who lead companies will ultimately be judged on whether they created exponential financial value—optimal value—for their shareholders.

Whether they do so, however, is determined by something very fundamental and yet so elusive to many. Their success will turn on

> allocating the responsibilities, risks, and rewards with those in its corporate ecosystem—employees, investors, consumers, clients, buyers, suppliers, vendors, advisers, and others—fairly, equitably, and transparently; and

> navigating the critical inflection points along the path they will inevitably encounter—successfully—continuing the ascending vector toward their optimal value.

The difference between managing these imperatives well enough and creating exponential financial value lies in the something intangible. It is in that something that often feels to corporate executives more ethereal. Some seem to have that magical ability to wrangle it to their benefit while it proves elusive to others.

The Craft enables you to capture this magic. It draws from those disciplines above the waterline—finance, law, operations, innovation, strategy, communications, and politics—while integrating that which dances from below—drawing from the insights revealed by Maslow, Skinner, Sun Tzu, Machiavelli, and an obscure theoretician named Clare W. Graves.

The Craft enables cross-correlation among underlying beliefs, values, attitudes, biases, motivations, and preferences and how these affect the corporate trajectory as a product thereof. It embraces techniques that stimulate reactions—responses sparked by the various underlying beliefs, values, attitudes, biases, motivations, or preferences (psychographics) of the actors. This response informs us as to how the actor perceives the allocation of reward, risk, and responsibility in their commercial exchanges.

Illustration 16

The insights and understanding obtained by using *The Craft* reveal everything that comes next for the company.

47

A POLITICIAN'S SECRET

There is another secret to making all this work,

Regardless of *whatever* corporate event, conditionality, or inflection point it is—a corporate spinout, financing, restructuring, resolving a dispute, structuring a tender, doing an acquisition, pursuing a major enterprise sale, launching a technology product, building new channels, or building an identity in the public marketplace;

regardless of *whenever* it will be experienced—one year out, a month out, a week out, tomorrow, or this afternoon; and

regardless of *wherever* it will be experienced—Silicon Valley, Dubai, Accra, Kiev, Munich, London, Singapore, Manhattan, Washington, DC, or Akron.

Always do this:

> *Run it like a campaign.*

Campaigns have an energy, a pulse, and a vitality. They are living organisms with behaviors that manifest outwardly as well as dynamics and influences determined by the deeper codes within.

Campaigns operate against finite deadlines.

They result in definitive outcomes, with clear winners and losers.

Campaigns, quite literally, determine everything that comes next.

But for the purposes of implementing *The Craft* as a practice, there is something deeper that makes the campaign the ideal model for managing complex corporate initiatives:

> *Whether you win or lose is based on how well you understand how people perceive, react, and think relative to the conditions they are experiencing.*

Those things above the waterline—the sales pitches, work plans, matrices of responsibility, financials, deal terms, legal structures, and strategic parameters—are all extremely important.

But it is those things that lie below the waterline—wired into how people perceive, react, and think—that move the needle.

This is one secret that we can steal from politicians. It is where the magic lies.

The art is in the intangibles; it is this art that separates those who create exponential financial value from those who do not.

Everyone will have a launch strategy; financial forecasts; messaging carefully crafted for the board, employees, and media; the policy analysis; the technical architecture; the brand strategy; the delivery model; the pricing analysis; and the legal review.

What virtually no else will do is the following:

1. Decrypt the philosophy, logical constructs, belief systems, and emotional responses—for their own team as well as for those sitting across the table—those key stakeholders highly influential to how your critical moment unfolds and what comes next.

2. Document the biases, patterns, and triggers of the individuals involved, both of your own team and of those sitting across the table.

3. Map where there will be resonance and people coming together and where they will be repelled.

4. Find the crack of light that will enable you to navigate successfully to the other side of the coming moment.

5. Build the right team with the skill and ability to evolve and adapt as critical inflection points dictate.

6.   Understand how new information, stimuli, and changing situational contexts are affecting your own biases, patterns, and triggers—affecting your own way of perceiving, reacting, and thinking.

7.   Develop a language and understanding of the methods being used across the team so that they understand the needs in the moment and are able to adjust quickly to support the team effort.

8.   Reverse engineer the timeline (T-30, T-21, T-14, T-7, T-0, or similar methodology) with key hurdles to be achieved along the way to increase your probability of success.

9.   Run it like a campaign—knowing that how highly attuned and effective you are in understanding how people perceive, react, and think will determine your success.

This is the path to creating asymmetric advantage over all others. It is the path to achieving optimal value. It will determine how you are remembered.

48

EXECUTION

This is a lot.

Very few—companies or executives—do anything like this. They fight from their heels in markets that move faster and more brutally, armed with new strategies, tactics, and weapons. They are unable to inflect their arc when it flattens, waiting until their egg rolls to the edge of the table and falls. They struggle to innovate, create, and break through when it becomes the imperative.

My company, Ironheart, helps companies and CEOs unlock their exponential financial value, including by

crafting the strategy, game plan, techniques, behaviors, and language used to pursue their optimal value;

building complex commercial ecosystems involving many diverse stakeholders with the ability to successfully achieve the targeted optimal value;

managing the dynamics and events of critical inflection points that inevitably will be encountered along the actual vector toward optimal value;

distilling the specific cross-correlations between the situational contexts faced by companies—either naturally or provoked by others—and the psychographic conditions they face with key stakeholders, influencers, and opponents in those moments; and

teaching corporate executives and their teams the fundamentals of *The Craft* and its application to increase their probability of success associated with critical corporate events, including new strategic initiatives, investments, enterprise sales pursuits, financings, M&A transactions, exits, tenders, procurements, disputes, restructurings, crises, policy initiatives, scaling up or scaling down, and the like.

We are entering a period of evolutionary change where the logical, predictable, programmable, and routine functions of technology, manufacturing, and distribution will increasingly be performed by machines and code. This shift will create an untapped reserve of potential—including of the creative, innovative, quantum, visionary, and empathic potential of the human mind, body, and spirit. To harness this potential—including through those companies that will usher in the future of how we live, work, consume, and contribute over the coming decade—we must unlock the deeper codes that will allow this potential to express itself most fully. We must empower individuals, teams, groups, and ecosystems to come together in ways that enable ideas to manifest at the faster and faster pace required of the times.

The Craft enables you to architect this journey.

You now know where to look.

You know what you are looking for.

You know what to do when you find it.